W9-ASB-024

WITHDRAWN

Illinois Central College
Learning Resources Center

REPRESENTATIVE
MEDIEVAL AND TUDOR PLAYS

VISITATION OF THE SEPULCHRE

From the Benedictional of St. Ethelwold
(c. 975)

REPRESENTATIVE MEDIEVAL AND TUDOR PLAYS

TRANSLATED AND MODERNIZED

With an Introduction by

ROGER SHERMAN LOOMIS & HENRY WILLIS WELLS

1887 - 1966, ed. and tr.

Play Anthology Reprint Series

BOOKS FOR LIBRARIES PRESS
FREEPORT, NEW YORK

PN
6112
.L 57
1970

STANDARD BOOK NUMBER:

8369-8202-9

LIBRARY OF CONGRESS CATALOG CARD NUMBER:

77-111109

PRINTED IN THE UNITED STATES OF AMERICA

Table of Contents

Introduction

MEDIEVAL DRAMA, both sacred and profane, was a new birth. The old classical tragedy had not been acted since 50 A.D. Comedy had degenerated into bawdy buffoonery, and then died out under the ban of the Church. Amphitheatres and arenas were converted into fortresses or fell into ruins. Professional entertainers continued to circulate century after century; they declaimed the Germanic epics, chanted the French *chansons de geste,* or recited the Arthurian *contes,* and inevitably they impersonated in voice and gesture the characters of their stories. But they inherited nothing from the drama of the ancients, and they originated nothing that could be called a play. Terence was read in the schools, but few had any notion that the speeches were intended to be spoken by several actors on a stage. When the nun Hrotsvitha of Gandersheim in the tenth century, and certain French poets in the twelfth, composed Latin comedies on the model of Terence or Plautus, they wrote for the closet, not the theatre. Even the meaning of "comedy" and "tragedy" was nearly lost; it was commonly assumed that both types were narrative, intended only for reading. Thus Dante called his masterpiece a *Commedia,* and Chaucer referred to his *Troilus* as a *tragedye*; neither learned author knew that these terms properly applied only to plays. The acted drama of antiquity had been dead for hundreds of years before the new acted drama was born.

When the drama of the Middle Ages came into being, three circumstances are worth noting. First, the Church, which had dealt the *coup de grâce* to the farces and spectacles of degenerate Rome, now watched over the cradle of the infant liturgical drama. Secondly, what we know of plays and dramatic spectacles up to 1400 indicates that with few exceptions they were composed and acted by amateurs. Minstrels and jongleurs, *mimi* and *histriones,* seem to have contributed little to the drama till late, either as authors or actors. Thirdly, the general rule holds (despite the exception of a few farces) that medieval drama is the product of successive applications of the universal histrionic impulse to pre-existing narratives or situations. This impulse, applied to the liturgical or Scriptural narrative, produced the mystery; * applied to the saint's legend, produced the miracle play; applied to the fabliau, produced the farce; and applied to the moral allegory, produced the morality. The miracle of the Virgin, the *pastourelle,* the *chanson de geste,* the exemplum, the Arthurian romance, the Robin Hood ballad, Petrarch's Latin tale of Griselda, and even the pseudo-Augustinian sermon on the prophets demanded and received dramatic form, thanks to this vitalizing impulse.

Though the medieval drama borrowed nothing from the classic drama, there were similarities in the circumstances of their birth; for both were born out of the intense emotions aroused by religious ceremonial, and both were born to music. The authorities seem to be agreed that Greek tragedy and comedy originated as songs sung at rural festivals. There seems to be general agreement also

---

* The terminology of medieval drama is confused. Medieval usage was extremely loose, and modern French and English scholars do not agree on the use of the corresponding words. We have adopted what seem to be the prevailing distinctions between the terms in Anglo-American practice. The word "mystery" (French *mystère*) does not have any connection with "mystery" (from Greek *musterion*) in the sense of hidden religious ceremony, nor with the obsolete "mystery" in the sense of trade or craft, but is derived from late Latin *ministerium,* a church service.

that the first medieval dramas were antiphonally chanted by monks during the office of matins in the candle-lighted choir on Easter morning.

The whole monastic community throughout Holy Week had been recalling in solitary meditation or commemorative ritual the central crisis of human history—the suffering and death of God made flesh. On Good Friday the veil of the temple had been symbolically rent in twain. The cross had been solemnly lowered, as if it were the sacred body, into the sepulchre represented by one of the altars. At the ceremony of *Tenebrae* on Thursday, Friday, and Saturday, the lights were one by one extinguished. Death seemed to have triumphed and man seemed doomed. Then on Easter morning what an overwhelming revulsion of joy when the cantors broke the silence of the darkened church with the single word, "Resurrexi!"—the word on which the fate of mankind hung. Thus it happened that, when the liturgy, prescribed in the sixth century, was elaborated in the tenth century by the addition of Latin lines set to music, called tropes, a brief dialogue in song was introduced before the "Resurrexi" of the Easter mass. The scene in the garden of Joseph of Arimathea was recalled by the words sung responsively, as if by the angels and the three Marys:

ANGELS: Quem quaeritis in sepulchro, O Christicolae?

MARYS: Jesum Nazarenum crucifixum, O coelicolae.

ANGELS: Non est hic, surrexit sicut praedixerat; ite, nuntiate quia surrexit de sepulchro.

In this trope and others very similar, found in manuscripts from St. Gall, Limoges, Vercelli, and Ravenna, the tidings of the Resurrection break forth into responsive song. But as yet there was no impersonation, no costume, no action, no *mise-en-scène*.

All these are found for the first time in the instructions for the service of Easter matins, composed by Bishop Ethelwold of Winchester, about 970. He probably set forth the current practice at Winchester, possibly modeled after that of the great house of Fleury on the Loire, to which he professes his obligation. His declared purpose was "the strengthening of faith in the unlearned vulgar and in neophytes." We may thus infer that the laity were admitted to witness the holy spectacle. Ethelwold's instructions are these:

While the third lesson [of matins] is being chanted, let four brethren vest themselves. Let one of these, vested in an alb, enter as if to take part in the service, and let him without being observed approach the place of the sepulchre and sit there quietly holding a palm in his hand. While the third responsory is being sung, let the remaining three follow, and let them all, vested in copes, bearing in their hands thuribles with incense, and stepping hesitantly in the manner of those seeking something, come before the place of the sepulchre. These things are done in imitation of the angel seated in the monument, and of the women coming with spices to anoint the body of Jesus. When therefore he who sits there beholds the three approach him like folk straying and seeking something, let him begin in a dulcet voice of medium pitch to sing: *Quem quaeritis* [*in sepulchro, O Christicolae*]*?* When he has sung it to the end, let the three reply with one voice: *Ihesum Nazarenum* [*crucifixum, O coelicola*]. To whom he [answers]: *Non est hic; surrexit, sicut praedixerat. Ite, nuntiate quia surrexit a mortuis.* At the word of this command, let those three turn to the choir and say: *Alleluia! resurrexit Dominus!* This said, let the former again seating himself, as if recalling them, say the anthem: *Venite et videte locum* [*ubi positus erat Dominus, alleluia! alleluia!*] And saying this let him rise and lift the veil and show them the place bare of the cross, but only the cloths laid there with which the cross was wrapped. Seeing this, let them set down the thuribles which they have carried into the same sepulchre, and let them take up the cloth and spread it out before the clergy and as if to show that the Lord has risen and is no longer wrapped therein, let them sing this anthem: *Surrexit Dominus de sepulchro, [qui pro nobis pependit in ligno.]* And let them lay the cloth on the altar. When the anthem is finished, let the Prior, sharing in their gladness at the triumph of our King, in that having conquered Death, He rose again, begin the hymn, *Te Deum laudamus.* This begun, all the bells are rung together.

This Visitation of the Sepulchre, the earliest liturgical play, was a spontaneous outburst of the dramatic instinct in the heart of the cloister; the inevitable overflow of the pent-up emotions of Passion Week in commemorative action, ending with the *Te Deum* and the triumphant peal of bells. For hundreds of years this theme, with variations and additions, was presented in the monastic and cathedral churches of Western Europe, and was performed in the chapel of Magdalen College, Oxford, as late as 1518, and at Angers in the 18th century. To the visit of the Marys at the empty tomb was added that of the apostles, and then the appearance of the risen Christ as a gardener to the Magdalen. In a twelfth century manuscript from Fleury we have a complete mystery play of the Resurrection, still retaining at its core the *Quem quaeritis* trope from which it had sprung.

Meantime, the Journey to Emmaus had also been dramatized, and was played on Easter Monday. The services of the Christmas season budded out into plays of the shepherds, the magi, and the slaughter of the innocents. Already in the twelfth century in the candle-lighted minsters, the angels sang, the shepherds knelt before the manger, the magi followed the star, and Herod tore a passion to tatters. All these liturgical dramas were composed and acted by the clergy in the sacred precincts; all were chanted in the Latin tongue. Their motive, in so far as it was not simply the human urge to act out that which is emotionally exciting, was to confirm and vitalize the faith.

The same mixed motives, doubtless, inspired the earliest miracle plays—enactments of the legends of the saints. The same twelfth century manuscript from Fleury which gives us the biblical plays of the Visitation of the Sepulchre, the Magi, and the Slaughter of the Innocents gives us also four plays of St. Nicholas, one of them specifically called a *miraculum,* an early occurrence of the word in the sense of a dramatized example of a saint's power. One of the St. Nicholas plays occurs also in abbreviated form in an earlier manuscript from Hildesheim, and we conclude that both forms are based on a common original of the late eleventh century. In 1087 the bones of St. Nicholas were stolen from Asia Minor by Norman sailors, and in their new resting place at Bari attracted pilgrims and Crusaders from all over Christendom. This event gave added impetus to the already popular cult of the Bishop of Myra, and he was adopted as the special protector of *clerici,* scholars young and old, because of his miraculous resurrection of three schoolboys, murdered by an innkeeper. Wace, writing about 1150, says: "Because he did such honor to the clerks, on this day [December 6] they hold a feast with good reading, good chanting, and reciting of his miracles." And as the bringer of good gifts to children Santa Claus has become increasingly beloved ever since.

It is possible that plays glorifying St. Nicholas were first composed for acting by boys in a monastic school, for Jacques de Vitry in the thirteenth century mentions "les enfants qui représentent S. Nicolas dans le récit de ses miracles." But of this there is no certainty, nor of the place where these earliest miracles were first performed. But, as with the early mysteries, the connection with the liturgy is still marked. Not only were the plays set to music and sung in Latin, but they ended with a portion of the mass or the office for December 6.

In a cultivated, rational mind these playlets evoke not reverence, but wonder that anyone could have taken them reverently. Possibly they were composed not only for, but by, juveniles. Speaking of the *Three Virgins,* represented in this collection, Professor Karl Young remarks: "One longs, indeed, for the courage to infer that the alacrity with which the suitors scent the dowries, and the uniformity of their wooings, are intended for comic effect! The solemnity of the plodding author's intention, however, is all too obvious." The St. Nicholas miracles can hardly be acted today except in the same spirit with which certain Victorian melodramas have been produced in our own time.

Two portentous innovations appear in the course of the twelfth century—the introduction of the vernacular languages, and the removal of the scene from the sacred walls. Whether these can be taken as symptoms of an inevitable drift or as partial causes of that drift, they undoubtedly show that the drama was becoming broader in its scope, more realistic, more secular. The first of these novelties is illustrated in this collection by the St. Nicholas play of Hilarius, which assigns to the "barbarian" rimed Latin stanzas, with repeated French refrains, such as; *"Des, quel domage! Qui pert sa chose, purque n'enrage?"* The author, who has left us, besides three plays, several Latin poems, evidently lived at one time in England, at another at Angers, and was one of the multitude who flocked to hear Abelard in the wilderness near Troyes (ca. 1125). He was a cleric of loose life, ready to turn his pen, now to pious advice, now to the flattery of a patroness, now to the praise of wine and beautiful boys, now to

sacred drama. He flourishes his classical learning; the
wine of Chalaustre surpasses Falernian; a certain *puer
Anglicus* is worthy to be a second Ganymede. Hilarius was
a typical goliard.

Though it has been suggested that he wrote his plays
for a troupe of wandering actors, yet two of them, *The
Raising of Lazarus* and *Daniel,* he evidently intended for
performance at matins or vespers. The liturgical connection was therefore preserved and the actors must have
been regular members of a religious community. But the
plays betray in more ways than one a secular note, an
increasing sophistication. The racy French of the "barbarian," his lashing of St. Nicholas, with tongue and whip
—these lowered the tone and emphasized the farcical element. In the *Daniel,* on the other hand, there is a striving
after grandiose effects—choruses of knights, Belshazzar's
feast with a display of glittering plate, and even a den of
lions! Though in the sonority of his rimed stanzas and
the verve of his dramaturgy Hilarius surpasses his predecessors, yet something is lost. The familiar story of the
invasion of the cloister by the world is here exemplified.

We have direct testimony to the secularization of the
drama in the twelfth century. Gerhoh of Reichersberg reveals that about 1122 the monks of Augsburg would consent to eat the meager fare of the refectory only when
some theatrical spectacle, such as Herod and the mas-
sacre of the innocents, was enacted there, and about 1161
he declares that certain priests are converting their
churches into theatres. Some twenty years later, Herrad,
abbess of Hohenburg, grieves that in many churches the
old solemnity of the liturgical plays has departed. "The
priests, after changing their clothes, go forth like a troop
of knights; there is no distinction between priest and
knight to be noted. At an unseemly gathering of priests

and laymen the church is desecrated by feasting, drinking, buffoonery, unbecoming jokes, play, the clang of weapons, the presence of shameless wenches, the vanities of the world, and all sorts of disorder." Herrad lauds those princes of the Church who forbid plays as tending to the dissolution of the faith.

And not in Germany alone did the divorce from the liturgy in spirit and in form occur. We have, to be sure, the testimony of William Fitzstephen about 1180 that London in his day, "instead of theatrical shows and scenic entertainments, has dramatic performances of a more sacred kind, either representations of the miracles which holy confessors have wrought, or of the sufferings in which the constancy of the martyrs was signally displayed." But a London where cock-fighting, bear-baiting, and rough-and-tumble sports were the vogue could hardly have been content with a drama so decorous as these words would imply. The *Jeu d'Adam,* written about 1180 in Anglo-Norman, shows the trend to secularization. Except for the Messianic prophecies in Latin, it is composed in French rimed couplets or quatrains. It was to be played outside the church, and the setting included a Garden of Eden and a hell. There are full stage directions, counsel to the actors (which anticipates Hamlet's), a good deal of hurly-burly provided by the devils, who, after they have carried off Adam and Eve in chains to hell, make a great smoke arise, shout in glee, "and clash their pots and pans that they may be heard without." And the devils seem to have provided an element somewhat betwixt the horrible and the hilarious throughout the succeeding ages of sacred drama. This play illustrates the linking of plays together which resulted in the great mystery cycles, for it presents not only the Fall of Man, but also the story of Abel, and a Procession of the Prophets. Most significant is the naturalness of the dialogue, the subtlety of Satan's strategy, and the clear differentiation of character between the pliant but humble Eve and the sturdier but self-righteous Adam. The liturgical play has clearly evolved most of the characteristics of the mystery.

While during the twelfth century both the scriptural play and the saint's play were tending to an elaboration and a sophistication which unfitted them for performance by clerics within a church, in the thirteenth purely secular dramas developed as the inevitable response to the increasingly profane spirit of the times. The *Roman de Ham* of Sarrasin relates in detail the great tournament held at Hem-Monacu in 1278, and sketches the dramatic scenes in which the Queen of France perhaps took the part of Guinevere, the Count of Artois that of the Chevalier au Lion, while "Sir Kay" and a lion provided occasion for Homeric laughter. Evidently in this instance Arthurian romance furnished the matter for courtly drama. A few years later Adam de la Halle, bourgeois of Arras, composed for the Count of Artois just mentioned his charming comic opera *Robin et Marion,* using the *pastourelle* as the basis of his plot. Written about the same time at Tournai, the farce of *Le Garçon et l'Aveugle* seems to be a dramatized fabliau. This can be surely predicated of the fragmentary English interlude *De Clerico et Puella,* based on the popular risqué story of the weeping bitch, derived from the Orient. Professor Grace Frank puts the case clearly: "It is evident that for the Middle Ages there was less distinction between narrative and dramatic genres than for us. When a poem was reworked so that its dialogued portions were spoken by a single jongleur, that was one type of entertainment. When a poem was reworked so that its dialogued portions were spoken by a group of jongleurs, the members of a *puy* or other society, . . . then the poem was presented *par personnages,* another type of entertainment resulted, and this we call drama."

Other marked developments of the thirteenth century were the emergence of a few professional authors as playwrights and the rise in France of the lay literary guild called the *puy* as producers and actors. Jean Bodel of Arras early in the century, besides writing a spirited version of St. Nicholas and the robbers, turned his pen to epic and to pastourelle. Adam de la Halle of the same city, mentioned above, was likewise a professional writer. Rutebeuf, Parisian author of a drama on the Theophilus legend and a satiric monologue of a quack pedlar of herbs, displayed an amazing versatility and power. In that vivacious society of northern France the professional author evidently found the composition of plays, sacred and profane, profitable.

Who were the producers and players of the new French drama, now so largely emancipated from the control of the clergy? There is little or nothing to show as yet the existence of professional actors. It is possible that Rutebeuf's *Dit de l'Herberie* was intended for mimetic recital by a jongleur, and there are several pieces in which rival jongleurs boast their wares, but these are not plays. So far as we know anything of courtly drama of the period, the parts were taken by members of the court. It was the prosperous bourgeoisie of Normandy and Northern France who sponsored and enacted the new emancipated drama. They created in the thirteenth century literary societies called *puys,* which not only encouraged public competitions in the lyric forms, but also on occasion produced plays, both grave and gay. It was probably the *puy* of Arras which gave the comedies of Adam de la Halle, and we have from the fourteenth century a collection of dramatized miracles of Our Lady and other pious tales such as *Amis and Amile* and *Robert the Devil,* which formed the repertoire of a *puy de Notre Dame* at Paris.

Similar bourgeois associations, devoted exclusively, however to the production of sacred dramas, came into existence toward the end of the fourteenth century and were called *confréries.* And to them we owe the great cycles of the Passion which are among the glories of fifteenth century French literature. These cycles are at the same time the natural culmination of the process of linking separate plays, and also furnish one more instance of the generalization that the medieval drama is the adaptation to scenic presentation by a number of actors of pre-existing narratives. The early *mystères de la Passion* show clearly their derivation from the *Passion des Jongleurs,* a narrative poem intended for public recitation. Bold were the spirits which attempted to present on an elaborate stage scenes in heaven and hell and the suffering and death of the Son of God. And though as poetry these plays are often long-winded and flat, like their English counterparts, as spectacles they must have possessed a certain majesty. The *mystère de la Passion* written about 1450 by Arnoul Gréban, choirmaster of Notre Dame, contained nearly 35,000 verses, numbered 220 characters, and took four days to act. The powerful appeal of such elaborately conceived and gorgeously staged dramatic festivals is demonstrated by the religious art of the fifteenth and sixteenth centuries, where quite obviously the grouping and the architectural settings have often been suggested by the stage. And that these dramas still have power to enthrall was demonstrated by the tense and awed silence with which in the summer of 1937 audiences witnessed scenes from the *Passion* of Gréban as they were enacted before the towering west front of Notre Dame.

Though the great cycles of the Passion, the old Testament, and of the Apostles are the somewhat formidable chefs-d'oeuvre of fifteenth century and early sixteenth century French drama, other types flourished. There were lengthy secular plays inspired by the heroism of the Maid of Orleans and the Destruction of Troy. Liturgical drama still maintained its traditions, and not until the Council of Trent (1545–63) was there a concerted effort to banish dramatic interpolations from the service-books. There were tediously instructive moralities, in which the familiar figures of religious allegory declaimed their prosy speeches, or even personified Phlebotomy and Pills recommended themselves as remedies for gastronomic excesses. There were *sotties,* political satires composed and acted by clerks; dramatized *exempla* showing the sufferings and the triumph of virtue; and numerous farces in which the taste of the vulgar for sheer obscenity and intrigue was shamelessly exploited. One supreme comedy stands out from this mass of mediocre or worthless work, *Maître Pathelin.* Composed about 1464 on the theme of the biter bit, it is rich in humorous situations, shrewd delineation of character, and racy dialogue. Not until the advent of Molière did French sense of form and French wit again display themselves to such advantage.

Typical of many tendencies of the time is a group of three plays composed by Andrieu de la Vigne in 1496 and acted under his direction in the Burgundian town of Seurre. The manuscript gives not only the names of the actors but also complete information about the production. The author was a facile versifier who turned out indifferently polemics, elegies, rondeaux, balades, and after traveling in the train of Charles VIII to Naples in 1494–95 wrote a poetic account of the expedition. A year later he was commissioned by the town authorities of Seurre to write a play in honor of their patron, St. Martin. In five

weeks he had composed an elaborate miracle, full of sen-
sational episodes, verbal acrobatics, and ingenious rimes;
and in addition had written two short pieces, a typical
farce at the expense of a dying miller and a devil who
mistakes his excrement for his soul, and a hybrid of miracle and farce, *The Blind Man and the Cripple*. Andrieu's
sources were literary: for the pious plays, the legends of
St. Martin; for the farce, Rutebeuf's fabliau, *Le Pet au
Villain*. The actors included some of the most substantial
citizens; no women or professional players took part.
There were mounted processions of the actors in gorgeous
costume, much blaring of trumpets, and solemn services in
honor of the patron saint in his church. Only one accident
marred the fête when Lucifer's costume caught fire as he
emerged from his hole. Otherwise the production was a
tremendous success. The farce-miracle, *The Blind Man
and the Cripple,* is included in this volume, partly because
of its own merits and partly because it was the inspiration
of Synge's *Well of the Saints.*

There can be little doubt of the exuberant vitality of
French drama in the early sixteenth century, but a very
great doubt of its artistic taste, its good sense, or its religious soundness. More and more the mysteries shocked
both the improving taste and intelligence of the Renaissance and the stricter religious standards of the Protestant and Catholic Reformations. They sank from the level
of great communal enterprises, encouraged by the Church
and patronized by the "best people," to the diversions of
the populace. In 1542 the parliament of Paris forbade
the production of the *Acts of the Apostles,* in a scarifying
condemnation. The actors were artisans who did not know
their ABC; their elocution was atrocious and produced
public derision in the theatre; they added apocryphal episodes and lascivious farces; the audiences on the way home

parodied their speeches and remarked mockingly on the reluctance of the Holy Spirit,—a dove, of course,—to descend. As a result, so runs the indictment, almsgiving and divine services suffered, and adultery, fornication, scandal, and mockery flourished. Six years later parliament took more drastic action and prohibited the representation of any sacred drama by the *confrérie*. The year 1548 marks the end of the medieval tradition in French drama.

Drama in the English tongue followed naturally upon drama in Anglo-Norman, and from the reign of Henry III to that of Henry VIII paralleled, though with considerable differences, the history of the various forms and their presentation in France. Just as the *Jeu d'Adam* furnishes a significant link between the Latin liturgical play and the vernacular mystery, so the early fifteenth century fragments, preserved at Shrewsbury but probably written in Yorkshire, exhibit the same transitional state. They supply parts of the dialogue for the Visitation of the Shepherds, the Visitation of the Sepulchre, and the Journey to Emmaus, and evidently are dramatic interpolations in the church services for Christmas, Easter, and Easter Monday. In fact, the manuscript gives the musical notation of the Latin words of the liturgy, to which the spoken words of the players were added. It is clear that these fragments belong to a drama which was still within the confines of the church and that the players were ecclesiastics who, as William of Waddington late in the thirteenth century informs us, "are permitted to give a presentation (provided that it be done chastely in the office of Holy Church, when one performs the service of God) how Jesu Christ, the son of God, was laid in the sepulchre, and how he arose, in order to increase devotion." On the other hand, not only does the introduction of speeches in English forecast the later mysteries of the market-place, but the speech of the shepherd at the manger is identical with that of the Third Shepherd in the York mystery cycle composed about 1350. It is written in the same rimed and highly alliterative stanzas and mentions one of those homely offerings to the Infant Christ made by the shepherds—a horn spoon that would "harbor a hundred peas." One could hardly ask for a firmer bridge between the chanted liturgical play and the spoken cyclic mystery than these Yorkshire fragments.

The dependence of the English, as of the French, dramatic tradition on non-dramatic literature is manifest. For instance, the Hegge cycle (abridged in this book) not only draws on the inevitable Vulgate, the apocryphal gospels, the *Golden Legend,* and Peter Comestor, but also on two English sources, *The Northern Passion* and Love's *Mirrour of the Blessed Lyf of Jesus Christ.* As Dr. Owst has emphasized—and overemphasized—many features of the religious and moral drama were simply transferred from the pulpit to the stage, and what had been declaimed by the preacher was performed by the player. At a later period the dependence of the drama on bookish sources is illustrated by Medwall's *Fulgens and Lucres*, which is based on a treatise on true nobility, printed by Caxton in 1481. John Heywood's *The Pardoner and the Friar* borrows freely from Chaucer. The Renaissance, however, shows a new tendency to adapt Dutch and French plays and gives a somewhat larger scope for original plots and themes.

Though England provided in the Middle Ages the chief types of dramatic spectacle, strange to say no pure example of the vernacular miracle based on a saint's legend has been preserved. *Mary Magdalene* (ca. 1500) might, of course, be so classified, but has been contaminated by farce and morality so that it is something of a hybrid.

But medieval and Tudor England enjoyed particularly the type known as the interlude. Originally it was the equivalent of the French *entremets* and was a piece, either short or divisible into parts, introduced between the courses to entertain the guests at a banquet. This meaning, long in doubt, is settled by the statement of Raoul de Presles (died 1374) to the effect that interludes "se font entre les deux mangiers," and by the discovery of Medwall's *Fulgens* (ca. 1497), clearly destined for performance in the intervals between three bouts of eating in Cardinal Morton's hall. Sometimes the word may have been used loosely to cover any short indoor play. The record of English interludes begins with the late thirteenth century fragment, *De Clerico et Puella,* and carries on into the reign of Elizabeth. They range in tone from low comedy to moralistic debate; in subject from saint's life to Protestant polemic.

But before 1500 the great bulk of English plays consisted of mysteries and moralities. Four great cycles of Scriptural drama, as well as a few smaller groups and single pieces, are extant. The authors of these mysteries, as their familiarity with religious literature suggests, must have been clerics. A monk, Ralph Higden, author of the Latin *Polychronicon,* seems to have had a share in the earliest form of the Chester cycle, performed in 1328. A Dominican friar composed the banns, or proclamations, for the Beverley plays in 1423. Less commonly clerics produced and acted the mysteries themselves. A satire of about 1350 ridicules the Franciscans for their performances: they hang one of their number on a green cross with bright leaves and blossoms; they fasten on him wings as if he were to fly; another comes down out of the sky in a gray gown as if he were a swineherd hieing to town; another friar stands in a cart made of fire, representing

Elijah. They all deserve to be burned! But in the main, the English mysteries of the fourteenth, fifteenth, and sixteenth centuries were sponsored and enacted by the laity.

Groups of citizens, associated in craft-guilds or religious fraternities, financed, produced, and played these dramas. Though amateurs in the sense that they were not actors by profession, these butchers and bakers and candlestick-makers were not amateurs in the modern sporting sense. The records of compensation to some of these actors make startling reading: To Fawston for hanging Judas 10d.; for playing God 3s. 4d.; to three white souls 5s.; to two worms of conscience 16d. Besides, at the rehearsals the performers were liberally served with refreshments: item for 9 gallons of ale xvii d.; item for a rib of beef and a goose vi d.

Each participating guild was assigned or chose a play to present, and sometimes a reason for the choice can be detected. At York in 1415 the shipwrights gave the building of Noah's ark, the fishermen and mariners the voyage in the ark; the goldsmiths and moneymakers played the Magi with their gold and their incense in costly vessels, the vintners gave the miracle at Cana, and the bakers the Last Supper. The cooks of Beverley, skilled with toasting prong and fire, gave a Harrowing of Hell in which, doubtless, there was a flaming hell-mouth and many a scorching soul. The guilds did not spare expense on costume or necessary properties, for the old account books solemnly record how much was spent on gloves for God, on Herod's blue satin robe, on wings for angels, on the pillar to which Christ was bound in the scourging scene, and for the stuff "to set the world on fire" on the Judgment Day.

In England the day set aside for these holy spectacles was sometimes Whitsunday or more commonly Corpus Christi Day. This latter festival, decreed by the Council of Vienne in 1311 to celebrate the miracle of the sacrament, fell seven weeks after Holy Thursday. The May or June weather was likely to be propitious for an outdoor performance, and since a procession of the Host, followed by the guilds with their banners, was prescribed by the Church, the townsfolk very naturally added the dramatic elements or converted the procession into a series of moving floats, which halted at the open spaces one after another, and served as stages for the plays. Thus, probably, the sporadic and unorganized enactments of sacred story in the thirteenth century, inspired by the liturgical dramas and the schoolboy miracles, became huge municipal enterprises, sponsored by the city fathers and attended at times even by royalty itself—the Corpus Christi plays.

When the histrionic talent of the guildsmen had been sifted by a committee to determine the best actors, the lines had been composed or revamped by some cleric with the requisite knowledge and a knack for riming, the rehearsals had been held, the costumes and stage-properties made, the assessments had been levied, and the municipal authorities had taken precautions against possible fracases and riots, then all was ready. Early on the sacred morning, after due observance of Mass, the players gathered at their pageants, as the stages on wheels were called; the spectators assembled at various open spaces. The first pageant, drawn by horses, creaked forth to the first station, and stopped while God the Father proclaimed Himself, Lucifer usurped His throne, and was ignominiously ejected. Then the first pageant rolled on to the second station for a repeat performance, and meanwhile the second pageant would take its place, and the divine Father created the world and its inhabitants. The third pageant in its turn arrived, and Adam and Eve in decorous white-leather tights were tempted and ate the forbidden fruit.

Thus, at each station the audience beheld the scenes of Man's fall and redemption successively enacted, and this was the common method of producing mysteries in England.

For anything as lively and popular as these spectacles were throughout nearly three centuries, there was no static uniformity. Other days than Corpus Christi are mentioned in the records. Sometimes an elaborate production occupied several days or a whole week. The Hegge cycle, as we have it, has evidently been transformed from a performance by guildsmen on pageants into a presentation by a large traveling troupe, on a number of fixed platforms about an open green. This type of staging, borrowed perhaps, though not necessarily, from the Continent, became increasingly common for outdoor performances in England.

The Chester cycle, which may retain some of Higden's composition in 1328, but is equipped with banns written for a belated revival in 1600, displays in spite of this long history a marked uniformity in stanzaic forms and in tone. Twenty-five pageants presents the drama of Man's fall and salvation with a certain simplicity and decorum, with few but welcome interruptions provided by Noah's scolding wife and her tippling gossips and by the natural antics of the Nativity shepherds.

The York cycle consists of forty-eight pageants and preserves a high level of dignity and much appropriate variation in verse and diction in accordance with the characters. Its editor assigns its composition to the middle of the fourteenth century, though of course it underwent some retouching.

The Wakefield plays (sometimes called after the Towneley family which once owned the manuscript, now in the Huntington Library, San Marino) are thirty-two in number, and several more have been lost. Five are simply corrupt forms of the corresponding York pageants. The transfer of these for use at Wakefield in the same county and the composition of the others cannot have taken place much before the middle of the fifteenth century when Wakefield first acquired a population and a prosperity sufficient to put through a large-scale enterprise. Thirteen of the extant plays are attributed to a highly gifted author, called the Wakefield Master; of these the *Secunda Pastorum* (the second of two alternative treatments which he composed on the visit of the shepherds to the manger) is his masterpiece. His characteristic verse-form (not reproduced in the modernized version of this book) is a 9-line stanza with strong anapaestic movement and an ingenious rime-scheme. To quote Professor Carey: "It is well adapted to dialogue and to natural conversation. . . . The long swinging quatrain at the beginning with its balanced internal rhymes serves for the presentation of facts and information; the more rapid tags and triplet drive them home or give the conclusion." Like Chaucer, the Wakefield Master seasons his style with homely saws; like Chaucer, he borrows freely from both "lered and lewed" sources, and reveals the genius in his selection. The sheep-stealing plot, for instance, is derived from a folktale which he alone had the wit to recognize as a delightful comic prelude to the angelic salutation and the adoration of the shepherds. Mak's pronouncement of a magic spell over his sleeping fellows is an effective piece of stage business, suggested probably by the *Four Sons of Aymon.* The dramatist carries further than his predecessors the differentiation of the shepherds and renders more plausible their behavior as Yorkshire yokels. Skillfully he forecasts the character of Mak in a line, and forecasts the development of the plot by Mak's prompt references to his wife's fecundity. No patron of the theatre needs to be told that the search for the sheep in Mak's cottage, the bafflement and departure of the shepherds amid Mak's sneers, their return in remorse of heart to bestow a present on Mak's infant, and their discovery that he has a snout, are perfect comic situations, perfectly handled. And Mak with his irrepressible boldness, fertility of resource, zest for acting a part, with his transitions from brazen effrontery to cringing self-exculpation, is a character both solid and subtle. The solidity and naturalness of the characters makes possible the transition from uproarious horseplay to the mood of kindly and cheerful reverence that pervades the later visit to the manger. These rough-spoken, rough-handed English peasants, with their shrewd comments on wages and graft, give a solid reality to the story of the Holy Night. They take nothing from its holiness as they jostle their way into the stable and kneel with humble gifts, with the reverence of poor and simple-hearted folk, before the miracle of the Divine Childhood.

The Hegge cycle, so far as the evidence goes, seems to emanate from Lincoln. Its old title, *Ludus Coventriae,* has no authority, and the N-town mentioned in the banns simply indicates that here should be inserted the name (*nomen*) of each town where it was acted when taken on tour. For unlike the other three cycles, the Hegge plays were performed not by local craft-guilds but by traveling actors. Though the manuscript is dated 1468, the work is the product of several revisions. On the whole the plays are more sober in tone than the other cycles. Noah's wife and the shepherds provide no comic relief, and the Devil, though prominent in many scenes, must have disappointed many spectators by his unwonted decorum. A commentator called Contemplacio furnishes a polysyllabic chorus.

There are compensations, however. Thirteen scenes from
the life of the Virgin are handled with great tenderness
and reverence; and on the other hand, a rough and caustic
satire is displayed in the pompous converse of the doctors
in the temple, in the taking of the adulterous woman, in
the trial of Joseph and Mary for fornication. The author
of this last scene has done a brilliant sketch of a contem-
porary ecclesiastical court, and has not minced his language.

The version of the Hegge cycle printed in this book represents about a third of the original, the rest being
omitted on grounds of taste or irrelevance to the main
theme of Man's fall and redemption. The scenes retained
are abridged somewhat, but keep close to the original
rhythms and the phrasing. It is hoped that in this form the
Hegge plays will demonstrate the inherent unity and
actability of a mystery cycle.

There was doubtless in the original presentation of the
mysteries with their ranting Pilates and Herods, their
leering and howling devils, their sometimes risqué situations, much to make the judicious grieve, even though it
made the unskilful laugh. We have already noted several
criticisms of irreverent or absurd presentations of sacred
drama. The first real piece of dramatic criticism in English is a Lollard tract "of miraclis-pleyinge" from the late
fourteenth century. The author regards all such performances as detrimental to the pure cause of religion. He resents an audience which derives merely emotional and aes-
thetic pleasure from scenes belonging, as he thinks, to
holy contemplation alone. Since, he argues, no normal
man would enjoy witnessing a play on the death of his
earthly father, why should a true Christian tolerate a
drama representing the death of his Heavenly Father?
The resentment expressed by the author was later deep-

ened by the harsh voice of Protestant revolt. A pageantry once very generally deemed pious came to be regarded with suspicion and hostility when not only the Catholic doctrine of the sacrament but also the ceremonials traditionally attending the feast of Corpus Christi became objects of violent hate. Thus the mystery plays and their pageant wagons, though they managed to survive into Elizabeth's reign, disappeared from England. The last of the guild actors were o'erdoing Termagant and out-heroding Herod in the provinces when Shakespeare's first plays were being put on in London.

Leaders of the twentieth-century theatre and even leaders in our modern poetry have returned to the study and the imitation of these plays all but forgotten for three centuries. A generation ago the most active minds in the theatrical world wearied of the literal and unimaginative technique employed on the "picture stage." Directors, such as Max Reinhardt, demanded a production more poetic, more imaginatively exciting, which the physical equipment of the modern stage made possible. The late medieval stage technique, with profuse symbolism, many settings, simultaneous actions, and operatic effects, once more was revived. As five centuries earlier, city squares were again filled with spectators, and façades of cathedrals served as imposing backgrounds for dramas of cosmic scope. Poets, too, in experimental mood, are now less inclined to raise the charge of doggerel against the "free verse" of the old plays. A notable return of interest in the simpler and more colloquial medieval style has been noted in many modern poets, such as W. H. Auden, Lewis MacNeice, C. Day Lewis, and John Crowe Ransom. The "sprung rhythms" of Gerard Manley Hopkins hark back to the popular versification outmoded by the classical Renaissance and seldom recalled in the Victorian period.

The mystery is not the only form of medieval drama successfully revived in the twentieth century; the long run of *Everyman* on Broadway proved the vitality of the morality. The earliest extant English example is *The Castle of Perseverance* of about 1405. Like the Hegge plays, it seems to have had its origin in Lincoln, but like them it was intended to be taken on the road by a troupe of professionals. Banner-bearers with trumpets were sent ahead the week before to collect a crowd and to advertise by poetic proclamation the merits and the contents of the coming play. For the performance a portion of the green was enclosed by a ditch, and within were erected five platforms and a large sham castle, open at the base. The long drama combines several familiar literary themes—the verbal contention of good and evil forces for the soul of Mankind, the old physical combat of vices and virtues derived ultimately from Prudentius, the arrival and summons of Death, the debate of the body and the soul, the pleading of the Four Daughters of God. Some lively action, borrowed from the courtly game of the siege of the Castle of Love, affords relief from the warfare of words. Three Virtues mounted on the battlements of the castle hurl down roses at the attacking Vices below, led by Belial with gun-powder burning in pipes attached to his hands, ears, and rump. The flowers prove more efficacious than the fireworks, and the Vices retreat, black and blue and bellowing with pain.

While the late fifteenth-century *Mankind* shows the morality performed in an innyard and degenerating into slapstick and obscenity, *The Summoning of Everyman,* which was translated from the Dutch at the same period, represents the English morality at its peak. It is a solemn, even majestic, treatment of the theme already employed in *The Castle of Perseverance,* and treated in art as the

Danse Macabre—the inevitable summons which awaits every mortal, and the vanity of reliance on friends, relatives, property, beauty, and strength in that dread hour. Good Deeds alone descends with Everyman into the grave. The play has become in a special sense international, pertaining to every nation as well as to every man. Hugo von Hofmannsthal's adaptation in modern German is best known today. But the English form, however rough in language and metre, still retains its power.

The interlude, of which we have many notices but no complete text before 1475, seems to have become more fashionable at the end of that century so that the lines were not only spoken in the tapestried banqueting halls of the great but also in many instances committed to print. As has already been observed, the tone of the interlude might be grave or gay, the matter might be derived from saint's legend or fabliau, so long as the play was adapted to the special conditions of the performance before the guests between the courses of a banquet. It must not be too long, or require too many actors, or offend the tastes of the particular company. *Fulgens and Lucres,* mentioned earlier, was played before the household of Cardinal Morton about 1497, and combines a main plot dealing with the counterclaims of highborn frivolity and comparatively lowborn valor for the hand of a noble maiden, and a farcical subplot on the amorous rivalries of the servants. In the Roman setting and the reminiscences of Latin comedy we detect the first signals of the Renaissance.

Though there is a strong anti-clerical bias in the works of the stout Catholic and friend of St. Thomas More, John Heywood, it was not with any controversial or didactic intent that Heywood wrote his merry interludes of *The Weather, The Four P's,* and the two included in this volume, but to entertain. All are brief, racy and topical,

the flowers of a happily unprofessional stage. Best known
of these is the *Four P's,* in which three rogues, a pardoner,
a palmer, and a 'pothecary, tell tall tales in a contest of
mendacity before a pedlar, who agrees to give the prize to
the greatest liar. The jesting is equally vigorous and
bawdy, but at times for us rather obscure. *John, Tyb, and
Sir John* is a farce with three characters long familiar to
the comic stage,—the ill-bred, insolent, and immoral wife,
the feeble, browbeaten husband, the lusty and profligate
priest. The stage business, though scarcely original, is
unsurpassed, and the dramatic aside is used with effect.
The researches of Professors Young and Reed have
uncovered the French origins of the play. Its inclusion in
the present volume serves, therefore, to emphasize a leading theme of this book—the cosmopolitan nature of
medieval drama.

The remaining interlude plausibly ascribed to Heywood,
The Pardoner and the Friar, is in subject a satire on the
abuses of the clergy, wherein it resembles *The Four P's;*
while in technique it resembles such a debate as *Witty and
Witless,* without being quite so literary and bare of theatrical vitality as that work. It is almost as witty as the
two other pieces which it resembles and far more dramatic
and hilarious. Indeed the mere reader may well be warned
of certain pitfalls in approaching this peculiarly actable
but unusual work. About half of it is composed of words
spoken simultaneously by its two leading characters. The
Pardoner occupies a pulpit on one side of the stage, the
Friar a pulpit on the other. Most of the time they address
the congregation, represented by the actual audience of
the play; the rest of the time they spit fire at one another.
When delivering their sermons, they speak, or rather
shout, together. This inclusion of the audience in the
magic circle of the play itself is typical of many medieval

spectacles, and is one of their devices most fascinating to the modern theatrical mind.

It is not the purpose of this volume to illustrate the forces which came to fulfilment in the work of Marlowe and Shakespeare, Corneille and Racine, to show the transition to the drama of the high Renaissance and the neoclassic era. The bridge is a long one and we shall not attempt to cross it. We shall grasp the true values of the older drama best if we do not think of it as "pre-Shakespearean," and realize it as essentially medieval—in its lofty aspiration and its coarse fooling, in its rude earthiness and its celestial vision. It can stand on its own merits. It was and is genuinely and brilliantly theatrical. Accordingly, this collection, by excluding all plays which suggest the Reformation and the humanistic revival, focuses attention on the intrinsic power of the medieval dramatic tradition; and by presenting certain notable examples of that tradition in a form intelligible to a modern audience, draws attention to the fact that they may be produced successfully at the present day.

ST. NICHOLAS, MURDER OF THE SCHOOLBOYS,
AND THEIR RESURRECTION

FATHER KNEELING BEFORE ST. NICHOLAS,
THREE DAUGHTERS, AND SON-IN-LAW

Font from Tournai, Winchester Cathedral

1129–71

The Miracle of
St. Nicholas and the Schoolboys

DRAMATIS PERSONAE

FIRST SCHOOLBOY
SECOND SCHOOLBOY
THIRD SCHOOLBOY
OLD MAN
OLD WOMAN
ST. NICHOLAS

SCENE I

FIRST SCHOOLBOY:

Led by a noble ambition, here we stand;
We've come to study in this foreign land.
But while the sinking sun still gives us light,
We'd better find a lodging for the night.

SECOND SCHOOLBOY:

Apollo's coursers now approach the brink
Of ocean, and beneath it soon will sink.
To us this country is entirely strange,
And so for lodging we had best arrange.

THIRD SCHOOLBOY:

What have we here? Though fast it's growing dark,
These lights reveal an aged patriarch.
Let's ask him and perhaps if we're polite,
He'll be our host and take us in tonight.

THE SCHOOLBOYS [*together say to the* OLD MAN]:

Good host, behold three schoolboys far from home,
In eager quest of knowledge thus we roam.

31

It's getting late, and would you be so kind,
Sir, as to take us in, if you don't mind?

OLD MAN:

God, who created all men, shelter you.
But as for me, I've other things to do.
I don't see where there's any profit in it.
You've come too at a very awkward minute.

SCHOOLBOYS [*to* OLD WOMAN]:

Dear lady, though it may be as you say,
That you'll gain nothing, won't you let us stay?
Perhaps God will observe the kindness done,
And send you as reward a baby son.

OLD WOMAN [*to* OLD MAN]:

Dear husband, in the name of charity,
Let us take in these boys, who seem to be
Respectable and studious as any.
We won't get rich, but we won't lose a penny.

OLD MAN:

I'll take them in, my love, just as you say.
[*To the boys*] Just as a favor, boys, come right this
way.

SCENE II

OLD MAN [*to* WIFE, *while* SCHOOLBOYS *are asleep*]:

Look at those purses, how they bulge! I swear
There must be quite a pile of treasure there.
Think, all that money could belong to us!
No one would know, no one would make a fuss.

OLD WOMAN:

Long as we've lived—too long it seems to me!—
We've had to bear the load of poverty.
Now here's a chance, if we are not too queazy,
To take the rest of life a bit more easy.

Where is your sword? Go, kill them where they lie;
And so from this time on shall you and I
Live like old Croesus. Do the job up right,
And God won't know what's happened here tonight.

SCENE III

NICHOLAS:

    I am a pilgrim, and the road is hard.
    I cannot drag my feet another yard.
    Therefore, as you do hope your souls' salvation,
    Grant me I pray a night's accommodation.

OLD MAN [*to* WOMAN]:

    Now what do you advise, beloved spouse?
    Shall I admit the old man to the house?

OLD WOMAN:

    He looks a most respectable old party;
    And so look sharp, and give him welcome hearty.

OLD MAN:

    Come in, come in, good pilgrim, come inside.
    For men like you we always can provide.
    If there is any nice dish you prefer,
    I'll do my best to get it for you, sir.

NICHOLAS [*seating himself at table*]:

    None of these things before me can I eat.
    Only one thing I want, and that's fresh meat.

OLD MAN:

    I'll cook you up a steak tender and hot;
    It isn't fresh, sir, but it's all I've got.

NICHOLAS:

    That is a lie, old man, come straight from hell.
    You have here in this house, I know right well,
    Meat that has just been slaughtered. Foul the deed,
    And foul the vice that led you to it,—Greed!

OLD MAN *and* OLD WOMAN [*falling on their knees*] :
>   Have mercy on us, mercy, we implore you!
>   O saint of God, see, we fall down before you.
>   Our sin is black as Satan's hide, but still
>   It can be pardoned wholly if God will.

NICHOLAS :
>   Bring here the bodies in their sad condition,
>   And let your hearts be smitten with contrition.
>   By God's grace shall these boys arise.
>   Go, mortify yourselves with tears and sighs.

NICHOLAS [*prays*] :
>   God, to whom sky and air and sea and land
>   Are only playthings in Thy powerful hand,
>   Those who now cry to Thee do Thou forgive,
>   And grant that these young scholars rise and live.

>   [*And afterwards let the whole choir sing:*
>   *Te deum laudamus.*]

The Miracle of
Saint Nicholas and the Virgins

DRAMATIS PERSONAE

> FATHER
> FIRST DAUGHTER
> SECOND DAUGHTER
> THIRD DAUGHTER
> ST. NICHOLAS
> FIRST SON-IN-LAW
> SECOND SON-IN-LAW
> THIRD SON-IN-LAW

FATHER:
> Groaning and grief have come upon us, in the stead
> Of all the happiness our former fortune shed.
>> Oh poverty!
> Alas and woe is me, the joys of life have fled!
> Good manners, beauty, youth, a famous name and
> old
> Are now worth nothing, less than nothing without
> gold.
>> Oh poverty!
> Alas and woe is me the joys of life have fled!

DAUGHTERS:
> When money leaves us, toil and misery come instead.
> See where our father mourns his desperate finances.
> Let's hope we still may live in moderate circum-
> stances.
>> Oh poverty!

Alas and woe is me, the joys of life are fled!
Come let us hear what plan he's hatching in his head.

FATHER [*complaining, to* DAUGHTERS]:

Dear daughters, you are now the only pleasure
Of miserable me, the only treasure
Of this your treasureless old father. Pray
Console me and advise as best you may.
Once I was rich, and now I am so poor
That neither day nor night I feel secure.
We'll suffer twice as much from this privation
As people who were born to lower station.
Little I care what penury may do
To me, but what will be the effect on you,
My darlings? How will hungry days and weeks
Transform your lively bodies, your full cheeks!

FIRST DAUGHTER [*to* FATHER]:

Dear father, do not sorrow sore;
By grieving you grieve us the more.
But listen calmly and take heed
To this design for which I plead.
We are so prostrate that perforce
We must adopt the only course
That's open. Thus to sell our beauty
Is now your daughters' bounden duty.
As eldest it devolves on me
To show my filial piety
Before my sisters, and I first
Must enter on the life accurst.
             O father dear!

             [*A bag of gold is thrown in.*]

FATHER [*joyfully, to* DAUGHTERS]:

Rejoice with me, rejoice, my darling daughters!
Farewell to all our poverty and grief!
Behold, this gold, miraculously brought us,

Will furnish instantaneous relief!
      O day of cheer!
DAUGHTERS [*standing, say*]:
    Now for this mercy let us raise
    A grateful prayer and joyous praise
    To God, and give to Him, the Giver,
    Laud, honor, glory, love forever!
      O father dear!
FIRST SON-IN-LAW [*entering, to* FATHER]:
    A gentleman, whose name none can disparage,
    I come to seek your daughter's hand in marriage,
      With your permission.
FATHER [*to* FIRST DAUGHTER]:
    Say, daughter, are you willing to espouse
    This youth of handsome figure, ancient house,
      And high position?
FIRST DAUGHTER [*to* FATHER]:
    My future in your keeping I have placed:
    Father, dispose of me to suit your taste,
      And I'll obey.
FATHER [*to* SON-IN-LAW]:
    Since this is so, to you I now confide
    My daughter. Let the nuptial knot be tied
      This very day.
      [*Exeunt* FIRST DAUGHTER *and* SON-IN-LAW.]
FATHER [*again lamenting, to* DAUGHTERS]:
    Dear daughters, you are now the only pleasure
    Of miserable me, the only treasure
    Of this your treasureless old father. Pray
    Console me and advise as best you may.
    Once I was rich, and now I am so poor
    That neither day nor night I feel secure.
    We'll suffer twice as much from this privation
    As people who were born to lower station.

Little I care what penury may do
To me, but what will be the effect on you,
My darlings? How will hungry days and weeks
Transform your lovely bodies, your full cheeks!

SECOND DAUGHTER [*to* FATHER]:

O father, do not add remorse
To make our misery ten times worse.
Do not make passing ills eternal
By plunging us in crimes infernal.
For well we know the heavenly portals
Are closed forever to those mortals
Who live in lust. Father, beware,
Or we their awful lot may share.
Do not, O father, do not force
Your daughters to this hideous course;
Or when we die, we'll plunge from earthly woe
Into the lake of endless fire below.

[*A bag of gold is thrown in.*]

FATHER [*to* DAUGHTERS]:

Rejoice with me, rejoice, my darling daughters!
Farewell to all our poverty and grief!
Behold, this gold, miraculously brought us
Will furnish instantaneous relief!
O day of cheer!

DAUGHTERS [*to* FATHER]:

Now for this mercy let us raise
A grateful prayer and joyous praise
To God, and give to Him, the giver,
Laud, honor, glory, love forever!
O father dear!

SECOND SON-IN-LAW [*entering, to* FATHER]:

A gentleman, whose name none can disparage,
I come to seek your daughter's hand in marriage,
With your permission.

FATHER [*to* SECOND DAUGHTER]:
> Say, daughter, are you willing to espouse
> This youth of handsome figure, ancient house,
>> And high position?

SECOND DAUGHTER [*to* FATHER]:
> My future in your keeping I have placed;
> Father, dispose of me to suit your taste,
>> And I'll obey.

FATHER [*to* SON-IN-LAW]:
> Since this is so, to you I now confide
> My daughter. Let the nuptial knot be tied
>> This very day.
>> [*Exeunt* SECOND DAUGHTER *and* SON-IN-LAW.]

FATHER [*again lamenting, to* THIRD DAUGHTER]:
> Little I care what penury may do
> To me, but what will be the effect on you,
> My sole remaining daughter? Till
> This fear is laid, I tremble still.

THIRD DAUGHTER [*to* FATHER]:
> O father, dearest father mine,
> Listen to me, no more repine.
> I'll give you now my counsel briefly:
> Fear God and glorify Him chiefly.
> Those who feared God, as you may read
> In Scripture, never were in need.
> The Almighty gave from Heaven above
> All things to all who gave Him love.
> Take heart, let not this destitution
> Affect your righteous resolution.
> See, from abysmal indigence
> Job swiftly rose to opulence.
>> [*A third bag of gold is thrown by* ST. NICHOLAS.
>> FATHER *falls at his feet.*]

FATHER:
> Stop, noble sir, whoever you may be,
> Stop and reveal yourself, for surely we
> Must thank you for this wondrous restoration
> Of our lost fortunes, and our souls' salvation.

NICHOLAS [*to* FATHER]:
> Nicholas is my name, but do not lift
> Your praise to me for this most timely gift.
> O brother, do not think that 'twas my hand that
>   poured
> This gold so lavishly upon you: 'twas the Lord!
>   [*Exit* ST. NICHOLAS.]

FATHER [*to* THIRD DAUGHTER]:
> Rejoice, my child, lift up your voice in gladness!
> Farewell to all our poverty and grief!
> Behold this gold, which now to all our sadness
> Will furnish instantaneous relief.
>   O day of cheer!

THIRD DAUGHTER [*to* FATHER]:
> Now for this mercy let us raise
> A grateful prayer and joyous praise
> To God, and give to Him, the giver,
> Laud, honor, glory, love forever!
>   O father dear!

THIRD SON-IN-LAW [*to* FATHER]:
> A gentleman, whose name none can disparage,
> I come to seek your daughter's hand in marriage
>   With your permission.

FATHER [*to* THIRD DAUGHTER]:
> Say, daughter, are you willing to espouse
> This youth of handsome figure, ancient house,
>   And high position?

THIRD DAUGHTER [*to* FATHER]:

My future in your keeping I have placed.
Father, dispose of me to suit your taste,
  And I'll obey.

FATHER [*to* SON-IN-LAW]:

Since this is so, to you I now confide
My daughter. Let the nuptial knot be tied
  This very day.

THE WHOLE CHOIR [*sings thus*]:

O compassion of Christ, worshiped with all praise,
who proclaims far and wide the merits of His
servant Nicholas, for from his tomb the oil flows,
and heals all who suffer.

The Miracle of
Saint Nicholas and the Image

by Hilarius

DRAMATIS PERSONAE

A BARBARIAN
FOUR OR SIX ROBBERS
ST. NICHOLAS' IMAGE
ST. NICHOLAS

First of all, the BARBARIAN, *who has gathered together his goods, comes to the image of* ST. NICHOLAS, *and commending them to his charge, says:*

All things whereof I am possessed
I've put here, Nicholas, in this chest.
Be thou their guardian, I request;
    Take of them good care.
Pray to my humble prayer give ear,
Look well that robbers come not near,
Unto thee I deliver here
    Gold and vestments rare.
To journey abroad is my design.
I to thy ward my goods consign.
When I return, see thou resign
    All again to me.
Now no more fears my mind beset,
Since in thy ward my goods are set.
Let me, returning, not regret
    The trust I put in thee.

When he has departed, some passing THIEVES, *seeing the door open and no guardian, bear everything away. The* BARBARIAN *returns, and not finding the treasure, says:*

> Out Harro! Murder, theft!
> Here all my wealth I left.
> The more fool I—'tis reft!
> > God! this is foul treason!
> If I be wroth, 'tis not without good reason.
> Treasures, at least a hundred,
> I placed here. How I blundered!
> Money and all are plundered.
> > God! this is foul treason!
> If I be wroth, 'tis not without good reason.
> 'Twas here I left my store.
> But here it is no more!
> This saint must pay the score!
> > God! this is foul treason!
> If I be wroth, 'tis not without good reason.

Then, approaching the IMAGE, *he says to it:*

> Here all my pelf I brought,
> And unto thee betaught.
> How like a fool I wrought!
> > Nicholas, hear!
> Give up my goods, or thou shalt buy them dear.

Taking up a scourge, he says:

> To thee I'll now impart
> A most improving art.
> Not lightly shalt thou part.
> Thou'rt in my power;
> Therefore the goods I left with thee restore.
> I call thy God to testify:
> If me thou'lt not indemnify,
> Thy knavish back I'll scarify.

Thou'rt in my power;
Therefore the goods I left with thee restore.
Then ST. NICHOLAS, *coming to the* ROBBERS, *says:*
Wretches, what is it ye do?
Short will be the hours and few
That ye gloat upon your prey.
It was in my custody.
Think not ye escaped my eye
When ye bore the spoil away.
Stripes I've suffered, without fable,
Since through you I was not able
To give back the treasure due;
Borne the assault of tongue and lip;
Nay, even more, the bite of whip.
In this pass I've come to you.
Speedily the goods restore
O'er whose safety I presided;
All was to my charge confided
Which by stealth away ye bore.
If ye do not this in sorrow,
Ye'll be dangling on the morrow
From the timbers of a cross;
For I'll openly proclaim
Your misdeeds and works of shame.
Therefore, haste, repair the loss.
The ROBBERS *in fear bring back all, and the* BARBARIAN
on finding them says:
Unless my sight's declining,
        They're mine once more;
Look, gold and jewels shining!
I marvel every moment more and more.
The lost are found again
        (They're mine once more),

Without expense or pain.
I marvel every moment more and more.
O true custodian,
      (They're mine once more)
Who hast returned each one!
I marvel every moment more and more.

Then approaching the IMAGE *and kneeling he says:*
Humbly I come to thee,
      Good Santa Claus!
Thou hast restored to me
What in thy keeping was.
Awhile I've been a rover,
      Good Santa Claus!
I now entire recover
What in thy keeping was.
My soul has gained new health,
      Good Santa Claus!
Since naught lacks of the wealth
That in thy keeping was.

Anon appearing to him, BLESSED NICHOLAS *says:*
Oh, pray not brother unto me.
To God alone make thou thy plea.
The same it is by whose decree
Were fashioned heaven and earth and sea
That hath returned thy precious hoard.
Be then no other than thou wast,
Adoring Christ both first and last:
Thy trust on Jesu only cast,
Through whom thine own again thou hast.
Mine is no merit nor reward.

In reply to him the BARBARIAN *says:*
Thy counseling I do not need;
For I'm determined with all speed

Each cruel wrong and loathsome deed
       To cast away.
I'll trust in Christ, God's only Son,
Who wondrous miracles hath done,
And all the law of Apollon
       Abjure for aye.
For Christ it is who by His hand
Hath wrought the sky, the sea, the land;
And yet to those who make demand
       His grace doth bring.
For Christ, the Lord of high degree,
Hath blotted out my sin for me.
So may His kingdom ever be
       Without ending!

The Miracle of
the Blind Man and the Cripple

by Andrieu de la Vigne

DRAMATIS PERSONAE

BLIND MAN
CRIPPLE
CLERICS
CROWD

BLIND MAN:
    Alms for one penniless and blind,
    Who never yet hath seen at all!
CRIPPLE:
    Pray, to the poor lame man be kind!
    With gout he cannot trudge or crawl.
BLIND MAN:
    Alas, right here I'll fade away
    Without a varlet to attend me.
CRIPPLE:
    I cannot budge, ah, welladay!
    Good God, preserve Thou and defend me.
BLIND MAN:
    That rascal who led me astray
    And left me here all empty-handed,
    He was a goodly guide, ifay!
    To rob me and then leave me stranded.
CRIPPLE:
    Alack, I'm in a pretty scrape!

How shall I win my livelihood?
I cannot from this spot escape,
However much I wish I could.

BLIND MAN:

Meseems I here shall fast all day.
Unless I find a varlet faster.

CRIPPLE:

Bad Luck has picked me for her prey,
And now she has become my master.

BLIND MAN:

For this desirable situation
Can't I get even one application?
I've had one varlet in my day
I trusted. He was called Giblet.
Jolly he was and on the level,
Though ugly as the very devil.
I lost a treasure when he left me.
Plague on the plague that thus bereft me.

CRIPPLE:

Will no one help me in my need?
For God's love, pity my estate.

BLIND MAN:

Who are you that so loudly plead?
Good friend, betake you hither straight.

CRIPPLE:

Alas, I'm planted in this spot,
Right in the middle of the street,
And cannot move. Saint Matthew, what
A wretched life!

BLIND MAN:

                Come stir your feet
Along this way: 'twill bring you luck.
Let's see what mirth we can discover.

CRIPPLE:

>Your tongue wags easily, my chuck.
>But mirth and joy for us are over.

BLIND MAN:

>Come hither; we shall make great cheer,
>An't please the Lord of Paradise.
>And though like blunderers we appear,
>We'll harm no man in any wise.

CRIPPLE:

>My friend, you throw your words away.
>For hence I cannot budge an inch.
>God curse them on the judgment day
>By whom I got into this pinch.

BLIND MAN:

>If I could walk in your direction
>I'd gladly carry you a bit—
>(At least, if I had strength for it)—
>To give you easement and protection.
>And you could succor me in turn
>By guiding me from place to place.

CRIPPLE:

>This is no plan to lightly spurn.
>You've said the best thing for our case.

BLIND MAN:

>I'll walk straight towards you if I can.
>Is this the right way?

CRIPPLE:

>   Yes, don't stumble.

BLIND MAN:

>Methinks it is a better plan
>To go on all fours and not tumble.
>I'm headed right?

CRIPPLE:

   Straight as a quail.
You'll soon be here in front of me.

BLIND MAN:

 When I come near you, do not fail
To give your hand.

CRIPPLE:

    I will, pardee.
Stop, you're not going straight, turn hither.

BLIND MAN:

 This way?

CRIPPLE:

   No, no! Turn to the right.

BLIND MAN:

 So?

CRIPPLE:

   Yes.

BLIND MAN:

   It puts me in high feather,
Good sir, at last to hold you tight.
Now will you mount upon my back?
I trow well I can bear the pack.

CRIPPLE:

 So much I must in you confide;
Then I in turn can be your guide.

BLIND MAN:

 Are you well set?

CRIPPLE:

   By Mary, yes.
Look well you do not let me fall.

BLIND MAN:

 If I should show such carelessness,
Pray God may evil me befall.
But guide aright.

CRIPPLE:
                    Yes, by my troth.
Look, here's my staff with iron shod.
Take it. And here I give my oath
To guide you faithfully, by God.

BLIND MAN:
Lord, had I known how much you weighed!
Wherefore is this?

CRIPPLE:
Plod on, good fellow
And keep the bargain that we made.
D'you hear? Get up!

BLIND MAN:
That's all quite well—Oh
But what a load!

CRIPPLE:
                    But what a lie!
A feather's not more light than I.

BLIND MAN:
Hold on, by God's blood; get a clutch,
Or else I'll drop you! Never yet
Did blacksmith's anvil weigh so much.
Get down; I'm in an awful sweat. . . .

                    [CRIPPLE *reluctantly gets down.*]
Hey, what's the news?

CRIPPLE:
                    What did you say?
They tell a really sumptuous thing.
A saint has lately passed away,
Whose works are most astonishing.
He heals the gravest maladies
Of which you ever yet heard speak—
That's if the sick are good and meek.
I here defy these powers of his.

BLIND MAN:

    What's that you're telling?

CRIPPLE:

              What's the joke?
It's said if the corpse comes this way
I should be cured all at one stroke,
And you too, likewise. Now I pray,
Come hither. If 'twere really so
That we were healed of all our woe,
Far harder then 'twould be to gain
Our livelihood than now.

BLIND MAN:

           Nay, nay.
That he may heal us of our pain
Let us go where he is, I say,
And find the corpse.

CRIPPLE:

          Were I assured
That we should not be healed by him,
Right well I'd go. But to be cured
And strong, I will not stir a limb.
No, we had better find our way
Out of this place.

BLIND MAN:

        What's this about?

CRIPPLE:

    Why, when I'm cured, I'll waste away
Of hunger. Every one will shout:
"Be off, and do some honest labor."
No, you'll not find me that saint's neighbor!
For if he fixed me up, they'll call
Me vagabond, and one would bawl:
"That brazen rascal, sound of limb,
The galleys are the place for him."

BLIND MAN:
>So glib a tongue I never saw.
>Yet I confess it speaks good sense.
>You have the gift of eloquence.

CRIPPLE:
>I tell you, I care not a straw
>To go and have the corpse remove
>My malady.

BLIND MAN:
>   Yea, 'twould be folly
>To seek it, and we will not move.

CRIPPLE:
>I dare pledge, if it cured you wholly,
>In a short time you'd feel regret.
>Folk would not give you anything
>But bread, and never would you get
>A tasty bit.

BLIND MAN:
>   May heaven bring
>Some great doom on my head, or let
>Them strip from off my skin
>Enough for two belts ere I'd set
>My eyes on it!

CRIPPLE:
>   Think, too, how thin
>Your purse would be.

BLIND MAN:
>Yea, that I trow.

CRIPPLE:
>Never a day but we'd be pining
>And there'd be not a penny to show.

BLIND MAN:
>Yea, truly?

CRIPPLE:
                By the Cross, I swear
    It will be even as I'm divining.
BLIND MAN:
    Since you have counseled me so fair,
    Henceforth your word I'll never doubt.
CRIPPLE:
    The body's in the church they say:
    We must not venture thereabout.
BLIND MAN:
    If ever we are caught in there
    May Satan carry us away!

                                        [*Pause.*]

CRIPPLE:
    Come, down this alley let us toddle.
BLIND MAN:
    Whither?
CRIPPLE:
            This way.
BLIND MAN:
                    Let us not wait.
CRIPPLE:
    My faith, 'twould show an empty noddle
    To seek the saint out in his lair.
BLIND MAN:
    Let us be off.
CRIPPLE:
                Which way?
BLIND MAN:
                            Why straight
    Where this old toper winters merrily.
CRIPPLE:
    A wise word have you spoken verily.
    Where go we?

BLIND MAN:

To the tavern. There
Without a lantern I can totter.

CRIPPLE:

I tell you, even so can I.
Give me an ale-house when I'm dry
Before a cistern full of water.

BLIND MAN:

Listen, I say!

CRIPPLE:

Listen to what?

BLIND MAN:

Whatever's making that todo?

CRIPPLE:

If it's the body!

BLIND MAN:

Horrible thought!
No longer we'd be catered to.
Hark!

CRIPPLE:

After it the whole town chases.

BLIND MAN:

Go look what's making all the pother.

CRIPPLE:

Bad luck is close upon our traces.
Good master, it's the saint, no other!

BLIND MAN:

Quick, let's be off: we must not bide.
I fear he'll catch us after all.

CRIPPLE:

Under some window let us hide,
Or in the corner of a wall.
Look out, don't trip!

BLIND MAN [*falling down*]:
>   The devil's in it!
>   To fall at such an awkward minute!

CRIPPLE:
>   Pray God he do not find us here:
>   Too cruel then would be our state.

BLIND MAN:
>   My heart is bitten through with fear.
>   We've fallen upon an evil fate.

CRIPPLE:
>   Lie low, my master, take good care,
>   And we'll crawl off beneath some stair.
>   [*Procession of clergy, bearing body
>   of saint in a reliquary, passes,
>   followed by crowd. Exeunt.*]

BLIND MAN [*looking at the reliquary*]:
>   I'm henceforth in this good saint's debt.
>   I see as never I saw before.
>   What a great fool I was to let
>   Myself be cozened into fleeing.
>   There's nothing, search the wide world o'er,
>   That to my mind's as good as seeing.

CRIPPLE:
>   The Devil take him in his chain!
>   He knows no gratitude nor grace.
>   Better if I had spared the pain
>   Of coming to this cursed place.
>   Alas, I'm quite at my wit's end.
>   Hunger will put me in my grave.
>   With rage I claw my face and rend.
>   Damnation on the whoreson knave!

BLIND MAN:
>   I was a very dunderhead
>   To leave the good safe road and tread

The doubtful bypath, wandering.
Alas, full little had I guessed
That clear sight was so great a thing.
Now I can look on fair Savoy
And Burgundy and France the blest.
Humbly I thank God for this joy.

CRIPPLE:

What an unlucky turn for me!
I never yet to work was taught.
This day has turned out wretchedly,
And I'm a wretch to be so caught.
So I am caught in Fortune's trap,
Not wise enough to dodge its snap.
Unfortunately I'm too wise
On my bad luck to shut my eyes.

BLIND MAN:

The rumor of thy power to bless,
St. Martin, has been spread so wide
That folk crowd in from every side,
This morning, toward thy holiness.
I thank thee not in Latin tongue
But in live French—thou art so kind.
If to thy mercy I've been blind,
Pardon I beg for this great wrong.

CRIPPLE:

Well, here I have a sweet new figure.
But you'll not have so long to wait
Before I'll manage to disfigure
This pretty form of mine once more.
I've stored up in this little pate
The use of herbs, and all the learning
I need to raise with oils a sore
Upon my leg, such that you'll vow
That with Saint Anthony's fire it's burning.

I'll make myself more sleek than lard,—
Don't think that I don't know the way,—
And there'll not be a man so hard
But will be melted with compassion.
Then too, I'm expert in the role
Of one whose body's one huge ache.
"In honor of the Sacred Passion,"
I'll quaver, "look at this poor soul,
And see these tortured members shake."
Then I'll tell how I've been at Rome,
How the Turks locked me up at Acre,
And how I'm here so far from home
On pilgrimage to St. Fiacre.

The Annunciation

Abridged from the Wakefield Mystery Cycle

DRAMATIS PERSONAE

GABRIEL

MARIA

JOSEPH

SCENE I

GABRIEL:

> Hail, Mary, most gracious,
> Hail, Maid of God, who art His spouse,
>> To thee I bow;
> Of all the virgins *thou* art queen,
> That ever were or shall be seen,
>> Men must allow.
> Hail, Mary, blessed one to be!
> My Lord of Heaven is now with thee
>> Beyond all end.
> Hail, woman who art without a peer!
> Good lady sweet, have thou no fear,
>> Thee I commend.
> For thou hast found alone
> The grace of God that was out-gone
>> Through Adam's plight.
> This is the grace that thee betides,
> Thou shalt conceive within thy sides,
>> A child of might.

MARIA:

> What is thy name?

GABRIEL:

> Gabriel,
> God's strength and His angel,
> Who comes to thee.

MARIA:

> Thou dost give me a greeting rare,
> To promise me a child to bear.
> How shall it be?
> I came not ever by man's side;
> I vowed a sinless maid to bide
> Since I was born.
> Therefore, I know not how
> This shall be broken for the vow
> That I have sworn.

GABRIEL:

> This is the truth to be:
> The Holy Ghost shall light in thee
> And His virtue
> Shall compass thee and work His will,
> Yet shall thy maidenhood not spill
> But aye be new.

MARIA:

> I love my Lord's command:
> I am His maiden for His hand
> And in His fold.
> I know the word that thou dost bring
> Will happen to me in each thing
> As thou hast told.

GABRIEL:

> Mary, sweet maid and friend,
> Behooves me now away to wend;
> My leave I take.

[Exit.]

MARIA:
>Fare to that Friend
>Who did to me an angel send
>For mankind's sake.

>>>>[*Exit.*]

SCENE II

JOSEPH:
>Almighty God, what may this be?
>Of my wife Mary I marvel me.
>>Alas, what has she wrought?
>Her body swells, she is with child!
>By me she never was defiled.
>>Of mine I know it's nought.
>I am full grieved with my old life;
>That ever I wed so young a wife,
>>That bargain must I ban.
>To me great grief 'twill surely bring;
>I might have known so young a thing
>>Would seek a man.
>She is with child, I know not how.
>In any wife, who would trust now?
>>In faith no man with wit.
>In all the world there's nought to do
>But go to her and ask her true
>>Whose child is it.
>>>[*He makes as if to go off, then turns*
>>>*back irresolutely.*] *
>Nine months I was from Mary mild;
>When I came home she was with child;
>>For shame, I must lament.

* In the original text Joseph here questions Mary as to her child.

I asked of women what had been;
They said an angel once was seen
      Since that from home I went.

"An angel spake with that fair wight,
And no one else, by day or night.
      Of that you're truly told."
They thus excused her verily
To make her clean of her follỳ,
      And fool me who am old.

Yet soothly if it so befall,
That she God's Son does bear, withal—
      If such grace might betide—
I know full well I am not he
Who is at all worthy to be
      That blessed one beside.

Nor yet in any company;
Unto the wilderness I'll flee
      Enforced to fare away;
Never again with her I'll deal,
But still from her I will steal
      Nor see her one more day.
              [*An angel appears on high.*]

ANGEL:
Joseph, give up and mend thy thought;
I warn thee well, thou must for nought
      Go to the forest wild.
Turn home unto thy wife again
Nor think in her to find a stain,
      For she is undefiled.

There is no wrongful work, believe;
In her the Spirit to receive,
    Who shall God's own Son bear.
Therefore with her in thy degree
Most meek and gentle look thou be,
    To her give all thy care.

JOSEPH:
    Ah, Lord, I love thee over all
    Who grantest me it should befall
        To guard that little child,—
    To me who had such evil thought
    And untrue blame on her had brought,
        On Mary, dear and mild.

    I grieve full sore for what I said,
    That her for sin I did upbraid
        Who had no guilt at all.
    Therefore to her now will I wend
    And praying her to be my friend
        On her forgiveness call.

                            [Exit.]

Scene III

JOSEPH:
    Ah, Mary, wife, what cheer?
MARIA:
    The better, sir, that ye are here;
        How long 'tis since ye went!
JOSEPH:
    In truth I've talked here like a fool
    Because I was both wrong and cruel,
        I knew not what I meant.

But I know well, dear wife and free,
I've trespassed against God and thee;
    Forgive me now I pray.

MARIA:

If ever ye did me belie,
May God forgive you, as do I
    With all the might I may.

JOSEPH:

Gramercy, Mary, thy good will
Sweetly forgives that I said ill,
    When I did thee upbraid.
'Tis good for him who has for wife
One meek as thou; for all his life
    He may hold him well paid.
Now light as linden leaf am I!
He that doth both release and tie
    And every wrong amend
Give me the grace and power and might
My wife and her sweet child of light
    To keep to my life's end.

      [*Exeunt* MARIA *and* JOSEPH.]

The Second Shepherds' Play
From the Wakefield Mystery Cycle

DRAMATIS PERSONAE

FIRST SHEPHERD (Coll)
SECOND SHEPHERD (Gib)
THIRD SHEPHERD (Daw), a youth
MAK
JILL
ANGEL
MARY

SCENE I

[*Scene a moor. Enter* FIRST SHEPHERD, *stamping his feet and blowing on his nails.*]

FIRST SHEPHERD:

Lord, but it's cold and wretchedly I'm wrapped;
My wits are frozen, so long it is I've napped;
My legs are cramped, and every finger chapped.
All goes awry; in misery I'm trapped.
By storms and gales distressed,
Now in the east, now west,
Woe's him who gets no rest!
We simple shepherds walking on the moor,
We're like, in faith, to be put out of door,
And it's no wonder if we are so poor.
Our fields they lie as fallow as a floor;
We're driven till we're bowed;
We're taxed until we're cowed
By gentry, rich and proud.

67

They take our rest; them may our Lady blast!
For their own lords they make our plows stick fast.
Some say it's for the best, but at the last
We know that's false. We tenants are downcast,
And always we're kept under.
If we don't thrive, no wonder
When they so rob and plunder.
A man with broidered sleeve or brooch, these days,
Can ruin anyone who him gainsays.
There's not a soul believes one word he says,
Or dares rebuke him for his bumptious ways.
He makes his pride and boast,
He gets his very post
From those who have the most.
There comes a fellow, proud as a peacock, now,
He'd carry off my wagon and my plow.
Before he'd leave, I must seem glad and bow.
A wretched life we lead, you must allow.
Whatever he has willed
Must be at once fulfilled,
Or surely I'd be killed.
It does me good, when I walk round alone,
About this world to grumble and to groan.
Now to my sheep I'll slowly walk, and moan,
And rest awhile on some old balk or stone.
Some other men I'll see;
Before it's noon I'll be
In true men's company.

> [*Enter* SECOND SHEPHERD, *not noticing*
> FIRST SHEPHERD.]

SECOND SHEPHERD:

Good Lord, good Lord, what does this misery mean?
What ails the world? The like has seldom been.
The weather's spiteful cold and bitter keen;

My eyes they weep, such hideous frosts they've seen.
Now in the snow and sleet
My shoes freeze to my feet;
No easy life I meet.
So far as I can see, where'er I go,
The griefs of married men increase and grow.
We're always out of luck; I tell you so.
Capul our hen goes cackling to and fro,
But if she starts to croak,
Our cock suffers a stroke;
For him it is no joke.
These wedded men have never once their will;
When they're hard pressed, they sigh and just keep
    still,
Groan to themselves and take the bitter pill.
God knows they've got a nasty part to fill!
And as for me I've found—
I know the lesson's sound—
Woe to the man who's bound!
Late in my life it still amazes me,
And my heart stops such miracles to see;
But yet when destiny drives, such things can be:
Some men have two wives, some have even three!
But if his lot is sore
Who has one wife in store,
It's hell for him with more!
Young men who'd woo, before you're fairly caught,
Beware of wedding! Give the matter thought.
To moan, "Had I but known!" will help you nought.
Much misery has wedding often brought,
And many a stormy shower.
You catch in one short hour
A lifelong taste of sour.
I've one for mate, if ever I read the Epistle,

Who's rough as is a briar and sharp as thistle.
Her looks are sour; her eyebrows, like hog's bristle.
She'd sing "Our Father" if once she wet her whistle.
And like a whale she's fat,
Full of gall as a vat.
I don't know where I'm at.

FIRST SHEPHERD:
Gib, look over the hedge! Are you deaf or no?

SECOND SHEPHERD:
The devil take you! Was ever man so slow?
Have you seen Daw?

FIRST SHEPHERD:
        Just now I heard him blow
His horn. I see him on the lea below.
Be quiet!

SECOND SHEPHERD:
        Tell me why.

FIRST SHEPHERD:
I think he's coming by.

SECOND SHEPHERD:
He'll trick us with some lie.

           [FIRST *and* SECOND SHEPHERDS *hide*.
           Enter THIRD SHEPHERD.]

THIRD SHEPHERD:
May Christ's cross help me, and St. Nicholas!
I've need of it; life's harder than it was.
Let men beware and let the false world pass.
It slips and slides, more brittle far than glass.
Never did it change so,
For now it's weal, now woe.
It's all a passing show.
Since Noah's flood, such floods were never seen,
Such dreadful winds and rains, and storms so keen.
Folk stammer or stand dumb with fear, I ween.

God turn it all to good! That's what I mean.
Just think how these floods drown
Us out in field and town;
No wonder that we're down.
We that walk at night, our herds to keep,
We see queer sights when others are asleep.
                    [*He spies the other shepherds.*]
My heart jumps. There I see two fellows peep,
Tall rascals both. I'll turn back to my sheep.
It was a bad mistake
This lonely path to take;
My toes I'll stub and break.
          [FIRST *and* SECOND SHEPHERDS *come forward.*]
May God save you, and you, O master sweet!
I want a drink and then a bite to eat.

FIRST SHEPHERD:
  Christ's curse, my boy, but you're a lazy cheat!

SECOND SHEPHERD:
  Does the boy rave? Let him wait for his meat!
  Bad luck now on your pate!
  The wretch, though he comes late,
  Would eat, so starved his state.

THIRD SHEPHERD:
  Servants like me, who always sweat and swink,
  We eat our bread too dry, that's what I think.
  We're wet and weary while our masters blink.
  It's late before we get to eat or drink.
  Grand dame and noble sire
  Delay and dock our hire,
  Though we have run through mire.
  But hear a truth, my master, for God's sake!
  A fuss about my appetite you make!
  But never supper gave me stomach-ache.
  Henceforth I'll work as little as I take;

Or I can run away.
What one buys cheap, they say,
Won't in the long run pay.

FIRST SHEPHERD:

A fool you'd be if you yourself should bring
To serve a man who'd not spend anything.

SECOND SHEPHERD:

Peace, boy! I want no more rude chattering.
Or I will make you smart, by Heaven's King!
Our sheep are they left lorn?

THIRD SHEPHERD:

This very day at morn
I left them in the corn.
They have good pasture, so they can't go wrong.

FIRST SHEPHERD:

That's right. Oh, by the Rood, these nights are long!
Before we go, I wish we'd have a song.

SECOND SHEPHERD:

I thought myself 'twould cheer us all along.

THIRD SHEPHERD:

I'm set.

FIRST SHEPHERD:

Tenor I'll try.

SECOND SHEPHERD:

And I the treble high.

THIRD SHEPHERD:

Then the middle am I.

[Then MAK *enters with a cloak drawn
over his tunic.]*

MAK:

Lord, of seven names, who made the moon that sails
And more stars than I know, Thy good will fails.
My brain is in a whirl; it's that which ails.
I wish I were in heaven where no child wails.

FIRST SHEPHERD:

Who is it pipes so poor?

MAK:

God knows what I endure,
A-walking on the moor!

SECOND SHEPHERD [*stepping forward*]:

Where do you come from, Mak? What news d'you
    bring?

THIRD SHEPHERD:

Is he come? Keep close watch on everything!
                    [*He snatches the cloak from him.*]

MAK [*with a southern accent*]:

I tell you I'm a yeoman of the King.
Make way for me! Lord's messages I bring.
Fie on you! Get ye hence!
This is no mere pretense.
I must have reverence!

FIRST SHEPHERD:

Why put on airs, Mak? It's no good to try.

SECOND SHEPHERD:

Or play the actor, for I know you lie.

THIRD SHEPHERD:

The scamp talks well, the Devil hang him high!

MAK:

I'll make complaint; I'll make you sizzle and fry!
I'll tell on you, in sooth.

FIRST SHEPHERD:

O Mak, ere you speak truth,
Take out your Southron tooth!

SECOND SHEPHERD:

The Devil's in your eye. You need a whack!
                            [*Strikes* MAK.]

THIRD SHEPHERD:

So you don't know me? I'll teach you better, Mak!

MAK [*changing his tune*]:

    God keep all three! What I said I take back.

    You're all good fellows.

FIRST SHEPHERD:

                Now you've changed your tack.

SECOND SHEPHERD:

    Why out so late, pray tell?

    Everyone knows right well

    You love roast-mutton smell.

MAK:

    I'm true as steel, as anyone will say,

    But I've a sickness takes my health away.

    My belly's in a parlous state today.

THIRD SHEPHERD:

    "The Devil seldom lies dead by the way."

MAK:

    As still as stone I'll lie,

    If this whole month have I

    Eat even a needle's eye.

FIRST SHEPHERD:

    How is your wife? how is she? tell us true.

MAK:

    She's sprawling by the fire; that's nothing new.

    The house is full of brats. She drinks ale, too.

    Come good or ill, that she will always do.

    She eats fast as she can,

    And each year gives a man

    A babe or two to scan.

    Though I had much more money in my purse,

    She'd eat and drink us to the Devil, sirs.

    Just look at her near by, the ugly curse!

    Will no one rid me of her?

    I'd give all in my coffer

    Mass for her soul to offer.

SECOND SHEPHERD:
> I swear there's no one so tired in this shire.
> I must get sleep though I take less for hire.

THIRD SHEPHERD:
> I'm cold and nearly naked; I'd like a fire.

FIRST SHEPHERD:
> And I'm worn out with running in the mire.
> Keep watch.

> *[Lies down.]*

SECOND SHEPHERD:
>   Not so, for I
> Must sleep. I'll put me by.

> *[Lies down.]*

THIRD SHEPHERD:
> Equal with you I'll lie.

> *[Lies down.]*

> Here, Mak, come here! Between us you must be.

MAK:
> You're sure you don't want to talk privately?

> *[Lies down, crosses himself and prays.]*

> And now from head to toe
> *Manus tuas commendo,*
> *Pontio Pilato.*

MAK [*while the* SHEPHERDS *sleep, rises and says*]:
> Now is the time for one who's short of gold
> To enter stealthily into a fold
> And nimbly work and yet be not too bold,
> For he might rue the bargain if 'twere told.
> He must be shrewd and wise
> Who likes his victuals nice,
> Yet hasn't got the price.

> *[Pretends to be a magician.]*

> A circle round the moon I here fulfill.
> Until it's noon or I have done my will,

You must each one lie there and be stone still.
To make it sure some good strong words I'll spill.
Over you my hands I lift;
Your eyes go out and drift
Till I make better shift.
Lord, but they're sleeping sound! All men can hear!
I never was a shepherd, but now I'll learn their gear,
And though the flock be scared, I'll creep right near.
This fat sheep with its fleece improves my cheer.
And now goodbye to sorrow!

[*Seizes sheep.*]

Though I pay not tomorrow,
I'll in the meantime borrow.

[*Exit* MAK.]

SCENE II

[*Interior of* MAK'S *cottage.* JILL *sits spinning.*]
MAK [*outside*]:
    Jill, are you in? Hello, get us some light!
JILL:
    Who makes this racket at this time of night?
    I'm busy spinning; I'll not stir a mite
    To get a day's pay. Curses on you light!
    It's thus a housewife fares.
    She's always rushed with cares,
    And all for nothing bears!
MAK [*outside*]:
    Open the latch, good wife! See what I bring!
JILL:
    I'll let you pull.

[*Opens door.* MAK *enters.*]

JILL:
        Come in, my own sweet thing!

MAK:
>Not much you care how long I stand and sing!

JILL:
>By your bare neck, for this you're like to swing!

MAK:
>I'm good for something yet;
>For at a pinch I get
>More than the fools who sweat.
>I had a lucky lot and God's own grace.

JILL:
>To hang for it would be a foul disgrace!

MAK:
>I've dodged before, my Jill, as hard a case.

JILL:
>Folk say that just so long a pot or vase
>To water it can come,
>Then broken it's brought home.

MAK:
>On that old saw be dumb!
>I wish that he were skinned; I want to eat.
>For twelve months I've not hankered so for meat.

JILL:
>Suppose they come here first and hear him bleat!

MAK:
>They'd catch me then. That puts me in a heat.
>Go bolt the door at back!
>I'd get from that whole pack
>The devil of a whack!

JILL:
>A good trick I have spied since you have none:
>We'll hide him in the crib till they have done.
>I'll lie and groan and say that he's my son.
>Let me alone to do what I've begun.

MAK:

> And I will say, tonight
> Of this boy you are light.

JILL:

> It's luck I was born bright.
> For cleverness this trick can't be surpassed.
> A woman's wit helps always at the last.
> Before they get suspicious, hurry fast.

MAK:

> If I don't get there soon, they'll blow a blast!

Scene III

[The moor. SHEPHERDS *sleeping. Enter* MAK.]

MAK:

> These men are still asleep.
> Their company I'll keep
> As if I'd stolen no sheep.
>
> > *[Lies down between them.]*
> > *[*SHEPHERDS *wake one by one, and cross*
> > *themselves.]*

FIRST SHEPHERD:

> *Resurrex a mortruis!* Here, take my hand!
> *Judas carnas Dominus!* I can't well stand.
> My foot's asleep and I'm as dry as sand.
> I dreamt we lay down near the English land!

SECOND SHEPHERD:

> I slept so well, I feel
> As fresh as any eel,
> And light upon my heel!

THIRD SHEPHERD:

> Lord bless us all! My body's all a-quake!
> My heart jumps from my skin, and that's no fake.
> Who's making all this din and my headache?

I'll teach him something! hear, you fellows, wake!
Where's Mak?
FIRST SHEPHERD:
              I vow he's near.
He went nowhere, that's clear.
THIRD SHEPHERD:
    I dreamt he was dressed up in a wolf's skin.
FIRST SHEPHERD:
    That's what too many rogues are wrapped up in!
THIRD SHEPHERD:
    While we were snoozing, seemed he did begin
To catch a sheep, without the slighest din.
SECOND SHEPHERD:
    Your dream has made you brood
    On phantoms, by the Rood.
    May God turn all to good!
                     [*Shakes* MAK.]
Rise, Mak, for shame! You're sleeping far too long.
MAK:
    Now may Christ's holy name keep us from wrong!
What's this? St. James! I can hardly move along.
I'm just the same, and yet my neck's all wrong.
             [SHEPHERDS *help him to his feet.*]
Thank you! It's still uneven
For I've been plagued since even
With nightmares, by St. Stephen!
I thought that Jill she groaned in travail bad;
At the first cockcrow she had borne a lad
To increase our flock. Guess whether I am glad!
That's more wool on my distaff than I had!
Woe's him who has no bread
For young ones to be fed.
The Devil crack each head!
I must go home to Jill; she's in my thought.

Just look into my sleeve that I steal nought.
I wouldn't grieve you or take from you aught.

THIRD SHEPHERD:

Go on, bad cess to you!

[*Exit* MAK.]

I think we ought
To count our sheep this morn.

FIRST SHEPHERD:

I'll see if any's gone.

THIRD SHEPHERD:

We'll meet at the Crooked Thorn.

[*Exeunt* SHEPHERDS.]

SCENE IV

[*Interior of* MAK'S *cottage.* JILL *at work.*]

MAK [*outside*]:

Undo this door! How long shall I stand here?

JILL:

Go walk in the waning moon! Who's shouting there?

MAK [*outside*]:

It's me, your husband, Mak. Hey, Jill, what cheer?

JILL:

Now we shall see the Devil hanged, that's clear.
I seem to hear a sound
As if a rope were round
His throat, and tightly bound.

MAK [*outside*]:

Just hear the fuss she makes for an excuse;
She doesn't do a stroke but to amuse.

JILL:

Who sits up late? Who comes and goes? Who
brews?

Who bakes? Whose hand knits stockings, tell me,
   whose?

                [Opens the door. MAK *enters.]*

It's a pity to behold,
Whether in hot or cold,
A womanless household!
But tell me how you left the herdsmen, Mak.

MAK:

The last word that they said when I turned back
Was that they'd count the sheep, the cursed pack!
They'll not be pleased to find a sheep they lack!
And so, however it goes,
They surely will suppose
From me the trouble rose.
You'll keep your promise?

JILL:

          Why, of course, I will.
I'll put him in the cradle, and with skill
I'll swaddle him. Trust in a pinch to Jill!
      [She wraps sheep and puts it in cradle.
                    Goes to bed.]
Come tuck me up. I'll lie here very still.
It may be a narrow squeak.

MAK:

Yes, if too close they peek,
Or if the sheep should speak!

JILL:

Hark, when they call, for they'll be here anon.
Let everything be ready. Sing alone
A lullaby, for I must lie and groan
And cry out by the wall on Mary and John.
You sing the lullaby,
And never doubt that I
Will pull wool over their eye.

Scene V

[The moor. Enter three SHEPHERDS.*]*

THIRD SHEPHERD:

    Good morrow, Coll. What's wrong? Why not
      asleep?

FIRST SHEPHERD:

    Alas that I was born! For this we'll keep
    A villain's name. We've lost a good fat sheep!

SECOND SHEPHERD:

    God save us! Who on us such wrong would heap?

FIRST SHEPHERD:

    Some rascal. With my dogs
    I've searched through Horbury Shrogs,
    Found one ewe of fifteen hogs.

THIRD SHEPHERD:

    Trust me, by Thomas, holy saint of Kent,
    'Twas Mak or Jill who on that theft was bent.

FIRST SHEPHERD:

    Peace, man, be quiet. I saw when he went.
    You slander him unjustly and should repent.

SECOND SHEPHERD:

    Though I may never succeed,
    I'd say it though I bleed,
    'Twas he who did the deed.

THIRD SHEPHERD:

    Then let's go thither at a running trot.
    I won't eat bread till at the truth I've got.

FIRST SHEPHERD:

    And I won't drink until I've solved the plot.

SECOND SHEPHERD:

    Until I find him, I won't rest one jot.
    I make this vow aright:
    Till I have him in sight

I will not sleep one night
In the same spot.

[*Exeunt.*]

SCENE VI

[MAK'S *cottage. Within* MAK *sings*, JILL *groans.* SHEP-
HERDS *approach the door.*]

THIRD SHEPHERD:

D'you hear them sing? Mak thinks that he can
croon!

FIRST SHEPHERD:

I never heard a voice so out of tune!

SECOND SHEPHERD:

Hey, Mak, open your door, and do it soon.

MAK:

Who is it shouts as if it were high noon?

THIRD SHEPHERD:

Good men, if it were day—

MAK [*opening door*]:

As much as ever you may,
Speak very soft, I pray.
Here is a woman sick and ill at ease;
I'd rather die than she had more misease.

JILL:

Go to some other place, I beg you, please,
Each footfall knocks my nose and makes me sneeze.

FIRST SHEPHERD:

How are you, Mak, I say?

MAK:

And how are you today,
And what brings you this way?
You're wet all through; you've run so in the mire,
If you'll sit down, I'll light you here a fire.

I've got what's coming to me. I'm no liar;
My dream's come true; a nurse I've got to hire.
I've more babes than you knew.
Surely the saying's true:
"We must drink what we brew."
Stay eat before you go; I see you sweat.

SECOND SHEPHERD:
Nothing will cheer us, neither drink nor meat.

MAK:
What ails you, sir?

THIRD SHEPHERD:
    We've had a loss that's great;
We found a sheep was stolen, when we met.

MAK:
Alas! Had I been there,
Someone had paid full dear.

FIRST SHEPHERD:
Marry, some think you were!

SECOND SHEPHERD:
Yes, Mak, just tell us who else could it be?

THIRD SHEPHERD:
'Twas either you or else your wife, say we.

MAK:
If you suspect us, either Jill or me,
Come rip our house apart, and then you'll see
That here within this spot
No sheep or cow I've got;
And Jill's not stirred a jot.
As I am true and leal, to God I pray,
This is the first meal that I've had today.

FIRST SHEPHERD:
Upon my soul, Mak, have a care, I say;
He's early learned to steal who can't say nay.

    [SHEPHERDS *begin to search.*]

JILL:

> Out, thieves, get out from here!

MAK:

> When her great groans you hear,
> Your hearts should melt for fear.

JILL:

> Out, thieves; don't touch my child! Get out the door!

MAK:

> Knew you her pangs, your conscience would be sore.
> You're wrong, I warn you, thus to come before
> A woman in her pain. I say no more.

JILL:

> O God, who art so mild,
> If you I e'er beguiled,
> Let me eat up this child!

MAK:

> Peace, woman, for God's passion, speak more low!
> You spoil your brains and terrify me so.

SECOND SHEPHERD:

> I think our sheep is slain. Think you not so?

THIRD SHEPHERD:

> We search here all in vain. We may well go.
> There's nothing I can find,
> No bone or scrap or rind,
> But empty plates behind.
> Here's no tame cattle, and no wild there is
> That smells like our old ram, I'll swear to this.

JILL:

> You're right; and of this child God give me bliss!

FIRST SHEPHERD:

> I think we've failed and that we've done amiss.

SECOND SHEPHERD:

> Dame, is't a boy you have?
> Him may Our Lady save!

MAK:

    A son a lord might crave.

    He grabs so when he wakes, it's a joy to see.

THIRD SHEPHERD:

    Luck on his buttocks! Happy may they be!

    But who god-fathered him so hurriedly?

MAK [*hesitating*]:

    Blest be their lips!

FIRST SHEPHERD:

                 A lie it's going to be!

MAK:

    Gibbon Waller was one,

    And Perkin's mother's son;

    John Horn supplied the fun.

SECOND SHEPHERD:

    Mak, let us all be friends again, I say.

MAK [*haughtily*]:

    It's little friendship you've shown me today.

    Goodbye, and glad to see you go away.

THIRD SHEPHERD:

    Fair words, no warmth—that's just as plain as day.

                 [SHEPHERDS *turn to go out.*]

FIRST SHEPHERD:

    Gave you the child a thing?

SECOND SHEPHERD:

    Not even one farthing!

THIRD SHEPHERD:

    Wait here; fast back I'll fling.

             [THIRD SHEPHERD *returns.* SECOND *and*

                 FIRST SHEPHERDS *follow.*]

THIRD SHEPHERD:

    To see your baby, Mak, I ask your leave.

MAK:

    No. Only insults from you I receive.

THIRD SHEPHERD:

Well, it won't make that little daystar grieve
If you let me give sixpence, I believe.

[*Approaches cradle.*]

MAK:

Go way; I say he sleeps.

THIRD SHEPHERD:

I think instead he peeps.

MAK:

When he wakes up, he weeps.

THIRD SHEPHERD:

Just let me kiss him once and lift the clout.
What in the devil! What a monstrous snout!

FIRST SHEPHERD:

He's birth-marked maybe. Let's not wait about!
The ill-spun cloth in truth comes foully out.
He looks like our own sheep!

THIRD SHEPHERD:

What, Gib! give me a peep.

FIRST SHEPHERD:

Where Truth can't walk 'twill creep.

SECOND SHEPHERD:

That was a clever trick, a shabby fraud!
The bare-faced swindle should be noised abroad.

THIRD SHEPHERD:

Yes, sirs, let's bind her fast and burn the bawd.
If she should hang, everyone would applaud.
Tucked in a cradle so,
I never saw, I vow,
A boy with horns till now!

MAK:

Peace, peace I ask! You'll give the child a scare.
For I'm his father and that's his mother there.

FIRST SHEPHERD:
> What devil is he named for? Look, Mak's heir!

SECOND SHEPHERD:
> Let be all that! I say, God give him care!

JILL:
> A pretty child is he
> To sit on woman's knee,
> And make his father glee!

THIRD SHEPHERD:
> I know him by his earmark, a good token.

MAK:
> I tell you, sirs, his nose in truth was broken.
> He was bewitched; so has a wise clerk spoken.

FIRST SHEPHERD:
> Liar! you deserve to have your noddle broken!

JILL:
> An elf took him away;
> I saw him changed for aye
> At stroke of twelve today.

SECOND SHEPHERD:
> You two are fit to lie in the same bed!

THIRD SHEPHERD:
> Since they maintain their theft, let's leave them dead.

MAK:
> If I do wrong again, cut off my head!
> I'm at your will.

THIRD SHEPHERD:
> Men, take my plan instead.
> We'll neither curse nor fight,
> But here in canvas tight
> We'll toss him good and right.

> [SHEPHERDS *exeunt, carrying* MAK
> *in a blanket.*]

Scene VII

[*Moor. Enter* SHEPHERDS.]

FIRST SHEPHERD:
    Lord, I'm about to burst, I am so sore!
    Until I rest, in faith I can't do more.

SECOND SHEPHERD:
    He's hefty as a sheep of seven score.
    And now I'll lay me down to snooze and snore.

THIRD SHEPHERD:
    Let's lie down on this green.

FIRST SHEPHERD:
    These thieves are rascals mean!

THIRD SHEPHERD:
    We'd best forget what's been.

                      [SHEPHERDS *lie down.*]
       [*An angel sings "Gloria in excelsis"; then
                         let him say:*]

ANGEL:
    Rise, herdsmen, rise, for now the Child is born
    Who frees mankind, for Adam's sin forlorn.
    To thwart the wicked fiend this night he's born.
    High God is made your friend. This very morn,
    To Bethlehem go ye;
    The new-born Deity
    In manger laid ye'll see.

                [*The* ANGEL *withdraws.*]

FIRST SHEPHERD:
    That was as queer a voice as ever I heard;
    Wonder enough to make a man be scared.

SECOND SHEPHERD:
    To speak of God's own Son of Heaven he dared,
    And all the wood I thought with lightning glared.

THIRD SHEPHERD:
> He said the baby lay
> In Bethlehem today.

FIRST SHEPHERD:
> That star points out the way.

> [*Points to star.*]

> Let's seek him there!

SECOND SHEPHERD:
> Did you hear how he cracked it?
> Three breves, one long.

THIRD SHEPHERD:
> Yes, and he surely smacked it.
> There was no crotchet wrong, and nothing lacked it.

FIRST SHEPHERD:
> I'd like us three to sing, just as he knacked it.

SECOND SHEPHERD:
> Let's harken how you croon.
> Can you bark at the moon?

THIRD SHEPHERD:
> Shut up and hark, you loon!

> [SHEPHERDS *sing off tune.*]

SECOND SHEPHERD:
> To Bethlehem he ordered us to go.
> I'm much afraid that we have been too slow.

THIRD SHEPHERD:
> Be merry, fellow, and don't croak like a crow.
> This news means endless joy to men below.

FIRST SHEPHERD:
> Though we are tired and wet,
> We'll hurry now and get
> Where Mother and Child are set.

> [*They start to walk.*]

SECOND SHEPHERD:
> We find by ancient prophets—-stop your din!—
> David, Isaiah, others of their kin,
> That God's own Son would someday light within
> A virgin's womb, to cleanse away our sin.
> Isaiah, don't forget,
> Foretold that one day yet
> *"Virgo concipiet."*

THIRD SHEPHERD:
> Right merry should we be that now's the day
> The lovely Lord is come who rules for aye.
> I'd be the happiest man if I could say
> That I had knelt before that Child to pray.
> But still the angel said
> The Babe was poorly arrayed
> And in a manger laid!

FIRST SHEPHERD:
> Prophets and patriarchs of old were torn
> With yearning to behold this Child now born.
> Without that sight they never ceased to mourn.
> But we shall see Him, now this very morn.
> When I see Him, I'll know
> The prophets' words were so.
> No liars were they, no!
> To men as poor as we He will appear.
> We'll find Him first, His messenger said clear.

SECOND SHEPHERD:
> Then let us hurry, for the place is near.

THIRD SHEPHERD:
> Ready am I and glad; let's go with cheer.
> Lord, if Thy will it be,
> Allow poor yokels three
> This happy sight to see.

ADORATION OF THE SHEPHERDS
From *Horae,* Printed by Vérard
Paris, ca. 1490

Scene VIII

[Bethlehem, a stable. The VIRGIN *seated, the* CHILD *on her knee. The* SHEPHERDS *enter and kneel.]*

FIRST SHEPHERD:

　　Hail, pure and sweet one; hail, thou holy Child!
　　Maker of all, born of a maiden mild.
　　Thou hast o'ercome the Devil, fierce and wild.
　　That wily Trickster now has been beguiled.
　　Look, how He laughs, sweet thing!
　　As my poor offering
　　A cherry bunch I bring.

SECOND SHEPHERD:

　　Hail, Savior King, our ransom Thou hast bought!
　　Hail, mighty Babe, Thou madest all of naught.
　　Hail, God of mercy, Thou the Fiend hast fought.
　　I kneel and bow before Thee. Look, I've brought
　　A bird, my tiny one!
　　Other faith we have none,
　　Our day-star and God's Son.

THIRD SHEPHERD:

　　Hail, pretty darling, Thou art God indeed.
　　I pray to Thee, be near when I have need.
　　Sweet is Thy look, although my heart does bleed
　　To see Thee here, and dressed in such poor weed.
　　Hail, Babe, on Thee I call.
　　I bring a tennis ball.
　　Take it and play withal.

MARY:

　　The Lord of Heaven, God omnipotent,
　　Who made all things aright, His Son has sent.
　　My name He named and blessed me ere He went.
　　Him I conceived through grace, as God had meant.
　　And now I pray Him so

To keep you from all woe!
Tell this where'er you go.

FIRST SHEPHERD:

Farewell, Lady, thou fairest to behold,
With Christ-child on thy knee!

SECOND SHEPHERD:

                    He lies full cold,
But well it is for me that Him you hold.

THIRD SHEPHERD:

Already this does seem a thing oft told.

FIRST SHEPHERD:

Let's spread the tidings round!

SECOND SHEPHERD:

Come; our salvation's found!

THIRD SHEPHERD:

To sing it we are bound!

[*Exeunt* SHEPHERDS *singing.*]
Here ends the Pageant of the SHEPHERDS.

The Mystery of the Redemption
Abridged from the Hegge MS.

[Sometimes Called the *Ludus Coventriae*]

THE SCENES

DRAMATIS PERSONAE

GOD THE FATHER

GOD THE SON

GOD THE HOLY GHOST

GABRIEL, also called the
SERAPH or GOOD ANGEL

AN EVIL ANGEL

LUCIFER, also called SATAN

ADAM

EVE

ISAIAH ⎫

JESSE

DAVID

JEREMIAH

SOLOMON

EZEKIEL

ROBOAM

MICAH ⎬ PROPHETS AND KINGS

ABIAS

DANIEL

ASA

JONAH

JOSOPHAT

ABDIAS

JORAS

HABAKKUK

AMON ⎭

CONTEMPLATION

AN ANGEL

TRUTH

MERCY

JUSTICE

PEACE

MARY

JOSEPH

BOSERACE ⎫

MANFRAS ⎬ THREE SHEPHERDS

MOIS ⎭

HEROD

BALTHAZAR ⎫

MELCHIZAR ⎬ THREE KINGS

JASPER ⎭

SENESCHAL

DEATH

LAZARUS

MARTHA

MAGDALENE

FOUR FRIENDS

JUDAS

GAMALIEL

REWFYN

LEON

ANNAS

CAIPHAS

PETER

A MESSENGER

THREE DOCTORS OF LAW

TWO WOMEN

PILATE

SIMON

VERONICA

FOUR JEWS	ARPHAXAT	
JESMAS, the Evil Thief	AMOURAUNT	FOUR
DYSMAS, the Good Thief	COSDRAM	SOLDIERS
JOHN	AFFRAUNT	
THE SOUL OF CHRIST	JOHN THE BAPTIST	
BELIAL	ABRAHAM	
A CENTURION	MICHAEL	
NICODEMUS	AN EVIL SOUL	
JOSEPH OF ARIMATHEA	A GOOD SOUL	
LONGEUS	THREE DEVILS	

NOTE: Since only six of the characters appearing in Act I appear in Act II, in a modern stage performance, as often in the old, seven-eighths of the actors in Act I could conveniently take new roles in Act II. The roles are all brief, only God speaking over a hundred lines and many actors having about a dozen or even less.

ACT I

Scene I

THE CREATION AND THE FALL

[*The scene represents Heaven on the spectator's left and Paradise on the right. Paradise is represented by an apple tree and a fig tree. Heaven is symbolized by a throne which consists of a simple stool placed on a small platform decorated with the rainbow.* GOD *enters. He wears a long robe and has a halo with three spokes symbolical of the Trinity.*]

GOD:

I am the true Trinity
Walking in this place;
Three persons in Myself I see
Closed within My face.
I am the father of sovereignty;
My Son is by My side;
My Ghost is Grace with Majesty;
In heaven We abide.
Three and one accord:
I am father of might.
My Son upholds the right,
My Ghost is lamp of light,
Of Grace the Lord.

[*He sits on His throne.*]

There was no beginning for Me to take,
And I am endless through My own might.
Now as a workman I commence to make
The high heavens and the stars of light.
In mirth and joy forever to awake,

I create in heaven the angels bright,
They shall be My servants and for My sake
With their mirth and melody worship My might.
I bless them with My bliss.
Angels in heaven forever shall be
Living in light eternally
With mirth and song to worship Me,
And no joy shall they miss.

> [*He leaves His throne.*]
> [ANGELS *enter singing the Sanctus.*]

LUCIFER:

In whose worship sing ye this song?
To worship God or to reverence me?
Unless ye worship me ye do me wrong,
For I am the worthiest that ever may be.

> [*The* ANGELS *divide into two choirs,*
> *the good and the evil.*]

GOOD ANGELS:

We worship God, most mighty and strong,
Who made us all, both us and thee;
We may never worship Him too long
For He is most worthy of majesty.
On knees to God we fall,
We worship Him eternally,
And in no wise do we honour thee;
A greater Lord there can never be
Than He who made us all.

LUCIFER:

A worthier lord, indeed, am I
And worthier than God I shall ever be.
I will therefore sit on His throne on high
As witness of my divinity.

> [LUCIFER *ascends the throne.*]

Above sun and moon and starry sky

I am seated now for all to see;
From God the father turn your eye,
And as your lord now honour me,
Sitting in my seat.

EVIL ANGELS:
Now God we utterly forsake
And as our duty undertake
To serve thee for thy honour's sake
And fall down at thy feet.

GOD:
Thou, Lucifer, for thy haughty pride,
I bid thee fall from heaven to hell.
And all the angels at thy side
Shall nevermore in heaven dwell.

Now I command you to descend
And never know our joy again,
But live in torment without end
In bitter burning, fire and pain
With everlasting night.

    [LUCIFER *leaves the throne, and with his*
        ANGELS *retreats to one side of the scene.*
        GOD *resumes his throne.*]

LUCIFER:
I do thy bidding, take my track
To hell, on heaven turn my back,
And change into a devil black
Who was an angel bright.

    [LUCIFER *and the* EVIL ANGELS *shed their*
        bright robes, appearing now as blackened
        fiends.]

And now to hell I take my path,
Where flames are burning fierce and steady.

I break my wind for fear and wrath;
In hell's dungeon my den is ready.
                    [LUCIFER *and the* EVIL ANGELS *plunge*
                                    out of heaven.]

GOD:

The first day and first night
The heavens are made for the angels' home;
On the second I make with all my might
The broad waves and heaven's dome.
The third day I bring to birth
Trees and every growing thing,
Flowers and herbs that bloom and spring,
Spangling and sweetly perfuming
The newly fashioned earth.

Sun, moon, and starlight dim
Upon the fourth day now I frame.
Next worms that creep and fish that swim,
Birds and beasts, both wild and tame.
The sixth day to my work I come
                            [*Here* ADAM *appears.*]
And make you, Adam by name.
Earth's paradise shall be your home,
Unless you spoil your bliss with shame.

Flesh of your flesh, bone of your bone,
                            [EVE *appears.*]
Adam, here behold your wife.
Of every beast be lord alone,
Of birds and fish, and every life.
Give them each their proper name,
Beasts and birds and fruit and flower;

All to you are mild and tame,
All the earth is in your power.
Name your wife as well.
Look that you do not cease
To give your kind increase,
All worship Me in peace
And do as I shall tell.

> [GOD *leads* ADAM *and* EVE *to the trees*
> *symbolical of Paradise.*]

Now, Adam, come forth to Paradise,
Where you shall have all manner of good.
All is made to greet your eyes
And all as yours is understood.
Here are fruits of every size,
Apples, cherries, pears and such,
Pepper and peonies, licorice and rice,
But the tree of wisdom you shall not touch.
All but this for you is wrought.
Here are all things which should please you.
Take your joy where all should ease you.
Eat not this fruit, lest death shall seize you,
For then you die, and escape Me not.
Heaven and earth, and beast and bird,
Now I have made all things of nought;
My blessing and My plighted word
I grant to all My hand has wrought.
My way to heaven is open wide,
On the seventh day I take My rest;
And all My creatures on every side,
And every kind shall now be blest;
On the seventh day let labour cease.
And all who halt their labour here,
Who hold the seventh day as dear

And worship Me, as shall appear,
Shall in heaven have endless peace.

> [GOD *returns to His throne.*]

ADAM:

Holy Father, blessed mayst Thou be,
For I can dwell in wealth enow,
I pluck fine dates abundantly,
The richest fruits fill every bough;
All this wealth is given to me,
And to my wife, mine own by vow;
I have no need to touch that tree,
Or in any fashion trespass now.
My gardening is good.
I know each fruit by name;
My work is but a game;
Indeed I were to blame
To show my Lord falsehood.

> [SATAN, *as* LUCIFER *is now called, enters disguised by a serpent's dress, and a woman's face. He picks an apple from the forbidden tree.*]

SATAN:

Hail, fair wife and comely dame,
Eat this fruit as I advise.
Take this apple and eat the same.
This fruit is best to make you wise.

EVE:

If I eat this apple I am to blame;
Our blissful cheer would turn to sighs;
We should die, be banished with shame,
And lose our place in Paradise.
God Himself has said
That day we eat the fruit we die;

Under God's own threat we lie;
Life from death must always fly
And this is what I dread.

SATAN:

Woman, if you take a bite,
Even as God is, so shall you be,
A wondrous wise and wily wight,
Like unto God in each degree.
Before your bidding, day and night,
All things shall stand obediently,
Sun and moon and heavens bright
Fish and fowl, by land and sea.
You shall be God's peer.
Here, this apple is for you!
Take it in hand and bite it through;
Then give Adam another too
And have no thought of fear.

EVE:

As wise as God is in each dispute,
And His fellow in cunning I fain would be.

SATAN:

Then say no more, but eat this fruit,
And learn if I speak faithfully.

EVE:

Since this indeed is wisdom's root,
I shall give it to Adam as you counsel me.
I shall eat; he shall follow suit
If God's peer in wisdom both may be
And equal to Him in might.
So to my husband I take my way;
Of this apple I'll make assay
And have him taste it too, if I may,
And take a hungry bite.

Adam, dear and darling man,

Listen, sir, to what I shall say.
Never think of heaven's ban;
Take good heart, and chew away.
Eat this apple as well you can,
And be God's peer in power and sway:
So through time's eternal span
Be strong and wise as God today
To fashion with your might
Fish and fowl, and sea and strand,
Bird and beast, water and land;
Take this apple out of my hand,
My dear, and eat a bite.

ADAM:

I dare not touch your hand for dread
Of our Lord God omnipotent;
I cannot do the thing you said.
Life is not given to us, but lent;
Eve, if we sin, we shall be dead;
Quickly, remember God's intent!
Don't eat, but throw it down instead,
And tremble at your hardiment
For dread of God's command!

EVE:

If you eat this apple here
You will become the Lord's own peer,
As witty and wise; so have no fear
To take this fruit in hand.

ADAM:

If we eat the fruit, my wife,
We kill ourselves, as God decreed.
I dare not eat and end my life
And can't agree to do this deed.

EVE:

A lovely Angel counselled me

To eat the apple without terror.
Like God I instantly should be
Mighty, wise and without error.
Surely this is sweet.

ADAM:

To have God's wisdom at command,
His mysteries to understand,
Here I take it from your hand:
Give me, and I will eat!

[*He eats the apple.*]

EVE:

Alas that ever that speech was spoken
Which the false angel said unto me!
Alas, our Maker's bidding is broken,
For I have touched His own dear tree!
The wrath of God has laid his stroke on;
Naked in sin ourselves we see.
The sorry apple has been the token
That brings to death my spouse and me.
Heavy is our sin.
Alas, our shame is clear and known!
Alas, that ever the apple was grown!
Dreadful death is now our own,
And now our pains begin.

[GOD *reappears in Paradise.*]

GOD:

Adam, whom My hands have made,
Where are you now? What have you wrought?

ADAM:

Ah Lord, through sin our blossoms fade.
I hear Thy voice, but I see Thee not.

GOD:

Adam, why have you sinned so soon,
So hastily to lose my boon?

I made you master beneath the moon
And lord of every tree.
Yet a single tree I left for My own.
Life and death therein are sown.
Your sin has cost you many a groan
And death you cannot flee.

ADAM:

Lord, I have worked against Thy will.
Myself I have not spared to kill;
The woman You gave led me to ill;
     She brought me to my bale.
It was her counsel and her creed.
She tempted me to do this deed,
Making me a beast, indeed,
     Naked without a veil.

GOD:

Woman, you who are this man's wife,
Why have you stirred this mutual strife?
Now you have lost your happy life,
     Doomed to death and sighs.
Foolish woman, say to Me
Why have you done this great folly
While I made you a great lady
     To play in Paradise?

EVE:

Lord, when Thou hadst left this place
A serpent with an angel's face
Promised us to be full of grace
     If we should eat that fruit.
I did his bidding, alas the day!
Death has caught us in his sway!
               [SATAN *reappears.*]
Satan, I see, has won his prey
     And bound us hand and foot.

GOD:

> Thou, serpent, with thy wicked wiles,
> Thy foul fables and false guiles,
> Thy deadly dart of sin defiles
>> Adam and his wife.
> Though they both have broken my word,
> Their worst of woe shall be transferred
> On thee, in hell to be interred
>> And nevermore win life.

SATAN:

> None the less you now may see
> Why I did this villainy.
> I am full of great envy,
> Of wrath and wicked hate,
> That man should live above the sky
> Where once I had my home on high,
> And now in darkest hell I lie
> Thrown out from heaven's gate.

GOD:

> Adam, because you had no dread
> To eat that fruit with hardihead,
> In sweat and labor earn your bread
> Until your life is furled.
> Go naked, hungry and bare-foot,
> Eat the herb, the grass, the root,
> And have all bitter bale to boot,
> A wanderer through the world.

> Woman, because you did this ill
> And bade your husband break my will,
> You shall be his servant still
> Obedient to man.
> Whatever he bids, look that you do,

Deep groans of childbirth pierce you through,
And dread and danger still accrue
Even to life's latest span.
Thou, wicked Satan, full of pride,
Foul envy follow at thy side,
Stealthily on thy stomach glide
Within a serpent bound
Until a maiden shall be born
Who shall leave thee all forlorn.
Thy head shall by her heel be torn.—
Now—creep upon the ground.

[SATAN *falls to the earth.*]

SATAN:

At Thy will I foully fall;
I creep into my stinking stall;
Hell's pit and heaven's hall
Shall follow Thy command.
I drop to earth; I quail and shake;
In horror of my fall I quake;
With my loss my spirits break;
My sorrow is at hand!

[SATAN *leaves.*]

GOD:

For the sin that stains you so
Out of Eden you shall go
And drag through life in toil and woe;
You'll taste of pain today.
For your sin and for your shame
An angel with a sword of flame
Shall drive you from your joy and game;
Your wealth has passed away!

[GOD *returns to His throne in heaven, while a*
SERAPH *enters and with a flaming sword*
drives ADAM *and* EVE *out of Paradise.*]

SERAPH:

Wretches unnatural and unwise,
Out of this joy hie you in haste.
With my flaming sword over Paradise
I drive you from bliss to care's sour taste.
Your mirth is turned in sorry wise;
Your sin has changed your wealth to waste.
For your false deed and sinful lies
I drive you quickly forth disgraced
To come herein no more,
Until of a maid a child is born
And on the cross is rent and torn
To save the joy you left forlorn
And all our wealth restore.

EVE:

Alas, alas, and wellaway
That ever I touched the tree!
I roam as a wretch on a rugged way;
In black bushes my bower shall be.
In Paradise are pleasure and play,
Fair fruits of fertility;
God's key has closed the gate today;
My husband is lost because of me.
Ah, my dear, you understand:
Now we stumble on stick and stone;
My mind is wild, my hope is gone;
Wring my neck and break my bone
With hardiness of hand.

ADAM:

Wife, your wit is not worth a rush,
Dear woman, change your thought.
I will not slay the flesh of my flesh
For from my flesh your flesh was wrought.
Our hap was hard, our wit was weak

When we to Paradise were brought.
Weeping shall be long fresh;
Short pleasure shall be long bought.
No longer tell your tale.
For if I should slay my wife
I slew myself without a knife,
In the lodge of hell to lead my life,
With woe in Weeping Vale.

But let us walk abroad in the land
Seeking our food with toil and care,
Digging and delving with hardened hand,
Stripped of our blessings, naked and bare.
And try, dear wife, to understand
How weaving guards our flesh from air,
Until some grace, through God's command,
At last release our long despair.
Now come away, my wife.

EVE:

Alas that ever we did this sin!
Now our fleshly ills begin.
You must delve and I must spin
And so sustain our life.

[They go out.]

Scene II

THE PROCESSION OF THE PROPHETS

[A procession of prophets singing led by ISAIAH *enters from the left of the stage and forms a line across the center like a row of figures across the façade of a church. A similar procession, also singing, led by* JESSE, *enters at the same time from the right forming a tier at a higher*

level. When the lines are complete the speaking commences.]

ISAIAH:

    Isaiah the prophet men call me by name,
Who breathe God's holy influence.
I feel the fire of prophetic flame
And say that a maid through obedience
Shall bear a babe to make resistance
Against foul Zebulon, the devil of hell.
He shall give man a stout defence;
In open field the fiend he will fell.

JESSE:

    Egredietur virga de radice Jesse
Et flos de radice eius ascendet;
A blessed branch shall spring from me,
Breathing a sweet and rosy breath.
Out of that branch in Nazareth
A flower shall bloom of Jesse's stem;
This flower by grace shall vanquish death,
And give mankind the diadem!

KING DAVID:

    I am David, the holy king,
Sprung from royal Jesse's seed,
And from my blood shall shortly spring
The blessing God has long decreed.
He shall come of royal breed;
A clean maid shall a mother be,
Defeat the devil's lying creed,
Conquer death and set men free.

JEREMIAH:

    I am the prophet Jeremiah,
According fully in every sense
Both with King David and with Isaiah,

Affirming before this audience
That God, of His benevolence,
From King and priest will take His line,
Buy us all from death's offence
And win us so a home divine.

KING SOLOMON:

I am Solomon, the second king
Who built the temple in its pride,
That young maiden figuring,
Messiah's mother, heaven's bride.

EZEKIEL:

A dream of this, well certified,
I, Ezekiel, have had also;
A gate is closed on every side
None but a prince may therein go.

KING ROBOAM:

The third sprout of Jesse's tree
As King Roboam men know me well;
From our kindred men shall see
A pure maid tread on the fiend of hell.

MICAH:

I, the prophet Micah, tell
All mankind that thus it is,
As mother Eve was of woe the well
So shall a maid be mother of bliss.

KING ABIAS:

I, King Abias, discern
The royal truth by these conveyed,
Declaring likewise in my turn
That all our mirth shall come of a maid.

DANIEL:

I, the prophet Daniel, am undismayed
For in promise of this I saw a tree:

All the fiends of hell shall be afraid
When maiden's fruit thereon they see.

KING ASA:

I, King Asa, believe all this;
God Himself will soon be born;
A maid shall bring us endless bliss
When rough on the rood he is rent and torn.

JONAH:

I, Jonah, say that on the third morn
He shall rise from death and bitter bale,
As figured in me who was once forlorn,
And three days lay buried within the whale.

KING JOSOPHAT:

I, Josophat, the sixth lineal sprout
Of Jesse's root, where all were bred,
Faithfully believe, without a doubt,
All that my progenitors before have said.

ABDIAS:

I, Abdias, foretell by God's bountihead
That after He rises from hell and pain
Death himself shall be damned and dead
And Life shall be granted in Paradise again.

KING JORAS:

And likewise I, Joras, numbered seven
From King Jesse's root, declare that He
After His Resurrection shall return to heaven
To be god and man there eternally.

HABAKKUK:

I, Habakkuk the prophet, agree
That when at length He is risen on high
He shall come as judge in majesty
To judge us all when we shall die.

KING AMON:

King Amon, I, by divine commission,
All truths which were said before resay;
Beseeching Our Lord for our sin's remission
And for mercy upon that dreadful day.
Thus all of us in our long array,
According in thought and will and place,
For our time of dying devoutly pray
That God will give us His gift of grace.

> [*The characters go out as before, re-
> peating their previous hymn.*]

Scene III

THE INCARNATION

[*Heaven, with* GOD's *throne, is on one side of the stage
where are gathered the* THREE PERSONS OF THE TRINITY,
FOUR WOMEN, TRUTH, MERCY, JUSTICE *and* PEACE, *as
well as* GABRIEL *and other* ANGELS. *On the other side of
the stage* MARY *kneels in a cottage at Nazareth reading
the psalter.* CONTEMPLATION *enters to speak the Prologue.*]

CONTEMPLATION:

Four thousand, six hundred and four years
Man has lain for his foul folly
In midst of hellish pains and fears
And is worthy to lie thus endlessly.
But this would defeat God's charity.
Good Lord, have pity on mankind's plight!
Remember Isaiah's prophecy
And let Thy mercy assuage Thy might!

SPOKESMAN FOR THE HIERARCHY OF THE VIRTUES:

Lord, may it please Thy high domination
To show pity to Thy creatures in misery!
Patriarchs and prophets have made supplication;
Our office is to present their prayers to Thee.
With angels and archangels, the third are we
Who stand in the first hierarchy on high.
For man, to Thy gracious majesty
Mercy, mercy, mercy we cry!

That Splendour, Lord, whom Thou madst so
     various,
Whose sin hath made him a devil in hell,
Moved mankind to be so contrarious.
Men mourned, but he forever fell.
His great malice, good Lord, repel
And take man again to grace;
Let Thy mercy make him with the angels to dwell
To restore Lucifer's ravished place.

GOD THE FATHER [rising]:

For all the wretchedness of all the needy
And for the poor men's lamentation
The rising of the Almighty shall now be speedy
And My time arrive of reconciliation.
In prayers My prophets have made supplication;
My contrite creatures for comfort sigh,
All My angels in heaven without cessation
For grace unto man continually do cry.

TRUTH:

Lord, I am Thy daughter Truth;
I must live forevermore;
To save these traitors would cause me ruth;
The offense of man hath grieved Thee sore;
And Thou hast promised once before

That Adam should die and go to hell.
And now to open heaven's door
Would bid to Truth a sad farewell.

MERCY:

O Father of mercy, Comforter of our days,
Who counselest us in every woe,
Hear Thy daughter, Mercy, who prays
For compassion toward mankind below.
He sorrows for sin's sad overthrow;
All heaven and earth for mercy cry.
Methinks he should not unpardoned go.
Such prayers and tears ascend the sky.

JUSTICE:

Mercy, I marvel at what you say!
I am Righteousness your sister, as well you may see;
God is righteous and right in every way,
Immortal man has wronged him grievously.
Therefore he shall be punished immortally.
For he forsook His maker Who made him of clay.
The devil for a master he chose, and he
Shall never be saved: nay, nay, nay!

PEACE:

Spare your speeches, sisters, as is fit;
It is not good for virtues to fight.
The peace of God overcomes all wit,
Though reason accords with Truth and Right,
Yet Mercy seems the best in my sight.
For if man's soul should abide in hell
Between God and man strife must alight.
And I with discord may never dwell.

Therefore, I hold you should rather accord
Than heaven and earth should so divide.
Place both your causes before Our Lord

And in His high wisdom let Him decide.
This is the peace which I have descried
And let us four live still together.
Alas, if man's soul forever died!
Or that one from the other of us should sever!

TRUTH:

In truth, I thereto give consent;
I will pray our Lord that it may so be.

JUSTICE:

I, Righteousness, am well content,
For in Him is perfect equity.

MERCY:

And I, Mercy, will never disagree
Till Wisdom has said that I shall cease.

[CHRIST *rises from His throne.*]

PEACE:

Here is God now, here is Unity;
Heaven and earth are pleased with peace!

CHRIST:

I think the thoughts of Peace, with evil unblended,
And this I judge to close your war:
If Adam had not died, Righteousness had ended,
And Truth also would be no more.
Truth and Right should hold folly sure.
Yet if another death come not, Mercy will fail,
And Peace be exiled forevermore.
So two new deaths must save you all.

He who shall die, as you must know,
Can harbor no iniquity;
Hell cannot hold Him fast below
Against His way to liberty.
Now find the champion. Search and see

Whose death can bring mankind's release.
Search heaven and earth industriously,
If you are pleased with such a peace.

TRUTH:

I, Truth, have sought the earth without and within
And, in truth, there can no one be found
Who is one day old and free from sin
Or who to this death will dare be bound.

MERCY:

I, Mercy, have run the heavens round,
And there is not one of such charity
Who for man would suffer a deadly wound,
I cannot tell how this shall be.

JUSTICE:

We are worthless servants, deep in shame,
Surely, I find us infidel!
His love must bear an ardent flame
Who dares for man to go to hell.

PEACE:

What God may do, no soul can tell.
Therefore, Peace gives this advice.
Let Him who gave counsel give comfort as well;
With God must lie the sacrifice.

CHRIST:

It pains Me that I once made man;
That is, I must suffer pain therefor.
Only a council of the Trinity can
Determine who may man restore.

THE FATHER:

Your wisdom, Son, made man of yore,
And in wisdom was his own temptation;
Thus you must ordain some plan therefor
To find how man may win salvation.

CHRIST:

> Father, He who shall do this must be god and man;
> Let Me see how I may wear that weed;
> And since in My wisdom he began
> I am ready to do this deed.

THE HOLY SPIRIT:

> I, the Holy Ghost, from You two proceed,
> Taking this charge at once on Me;
> I, Love, to Your lover shall give You speed:
> This is the consent of Our Unity.

> > [*The* FOUR VIRTUES *embrace one another.*]

THE FATHER:

> Go, Angel Gabriel, as Our breath
> Into the country of Galilee;
> The name of the city is Nazareth;
> A wedded maiden you shall see
> The wife of Joseph, and verily
> She is of the house which David bore.
> The name of this maid of glee
> Is Mary, who shall all restore.

CHRIST:

> Say that she is sinless and full of grace,
> And that I, the Son of God, shall be her son;
> Hasten that you may arrive apace,
> Or I shall be present ere you have begun.
> I have great haste to see this done,
> And to be born of a maid whom spirits adore.
> Tell her that by her is won
> All which your angels lost before.

THE HOLY SPIRIT:

> And if she ask how it may be,
> Tell her that I, the Holy Ghost, do this;
> She shall be saved through Our Unity.
> In token, her barren cousin Elizabeth is

Quick with child in her old age, ywis.
Tell her nothing is impossible for God to do.
Her body shall be so filled with bliss
She shall soon believe this message true.

GABRIEL:

On this high embassy, Lord, I shall fly,
It shall be done even as a thought;
Behold, dear God, how true am I,
I take my flight, and linger not!

[GABRIEL *passes from Heaven to
the house of* MARY.]

Ave Maria, gratia plena. Dominus tecum.
Hail full of grace! God is with thee, I say!
Among all women blessed art thou!
Here the name Eva is turned to Ave,
That is to say, without sorrow, as thou art now.

MARY:

Ah, merciful God, this is a marvellous greeting!
The angel's words are dreadful to hear.
I am much troubled by this strange meeting.
Angels indeed daily appear
But not in form of man, and that is my fear.
Also to be given so high a name,
When I am unworthy of this heavenly cheer,
Gives me much dread and greater shame.

GABRIEL:

Mary, for this have no dread,
For God's grace has fallen on thee.
Thou shalt conceive and in maidenhead
Bear the Son of the Trinity,
And Jesus His blessed name shall be.
He shall be great, the son of the highest, the angels'
    friend;
The Lord shall give him his father David's see,

Reigning in the house of Jacob whose reign shall
have no end.

MARY:

Angel, I ask you now
In what manner this thing can be?
As for knowledge of man, I have none now;
I ever have kept, and ever shall keep, virginity.
I cannot doubt what you say to me
But I ask, so that I may know—

GABRIEL:

From on high the Holy Ghost shall fall on thee
And the virtue of the Highest shall shadow so.
Of the holy Spirit thou shalt shortly bear
God's Son, who shall be called the Sapient One.
And see, thy cousin Elizabeth there
In her old age has conceived a son.
Her six months of bearing have run,
Her barrenness has passed away.—
Nothing is impossible which God will have done:
We listen to hear what thou wilt say.

[*A pause.*]

Mary, come and haste thee,
And take at once good heed
How the Holy Ghost in Trinity
Awaits assent to grant His meed.
Through wise work of divinity
The Second Person comes indeed
To be man by fraternity
Born of thy gracious seed.

They too are expectant for a space,
The blessed spirits, who have the view
Of heavenly joy and God's own face;
And all the mortals good and true

Who habit in this earthly place;
And all thy kindred, who foreknew,
And all the chosen souls of grace
Who are in hell, but hope anew.

As Adam, Abraham, and David the seer,
And many others of good reputation;
All pause in praise of God to hear
Thine answer to the incarnation;
Thou must preserve us all from fear
And grant to all mankind salvation.
Give me my answer now, lady dear,
And grant these creatures consolation.

MARY:

With all meekness I incline to their accord,
Bowing down my face with all benignity.
See here the handmaid of our Lord:
According to thy word, be it done to me!

GABRIEL:

Gramercy, my lady free,
Gramercy for thy word of might,
Gramercy for thy great humility,
Gramercy, thou lantern of light!

> [*Here* THE HOLY GHOST *descends with three
> beams of light to* OUR LADY; THE SON OF
> GOD *shines with three beams upon* THE HOLY
> GHOST, *and* GOD THE FATHER *with three
> beams upon* THE SON. *And so all three enter
> her bosom.*]

MARY:

Ah, now I feel in the body of me
Perfect God and perfect man;
And the form of a child's carnality
And all at once, thus God began.

I cannot tell what joy and bliss
I find through all my body fly;
Angel Gabriel, I thank thee for this;
Most meekly commend me to my Father on high.

GABRIEL:

At thy will, Lady, it shall be,
Thou gentlest of blood, and highest of race,
Reigning on earth in any degree
Through the high occasion of heaven's grace.
I commend myself to thee, throne of the Trinity,
O mother of Jesus, and meekest maid!
Queen of heaven, lady of earth, empress of hell,
these three,
And succor of the sinful who cry for aid.
Through thy blessed body our bliss is remade,
To thee, mother of mercy, I humbly cry!
And as I began, with an Ave I fade,
Joining heaven to earth, and ascend on high.

[THE ANGELS *in heaven sing the sequence: Ave
Maria, gratia plena; Dominus tecum, virgo
serena.*]

Scene IV

THE CHERRY TREE

[*On the road to Bethlehem. A bare tree on one side of
the stage. Enter* MARY *and* JOSEPH *travelling to Bethlehem.*]

JOSEPH:

Lord, what trouble is made for man!
Rest in this world is given to none
For our lord and Emperor Octavian
Demands a tribute from every one.

In every city the order's the same.
I, a poor carpenter of David's kin,
Must obey the commandment or fall in sin,
Coming to bitter blame.
Now, Mary, my wife, what have you to say?
For I must surely go from you
To the city of Bethlehem far away;
The journey is hard and the comforts few.

MARY:

My husband, I will take it too,
For there live some of my family.
Bethlehem is a city I long to view
And my friends will be a great joy to me.

JOSEPH:

Wife, think of your baby; I greatly fear
That you would suffer crossing the wild.
You know I would gladly give you cheer,—
Though women are moody whenever with child.
But come, let us go as fast as you may,
And Almighty God speed us upon our way.

MARY:

Ah, my sweet husband, what do I see?
What tree is standing upon that hill?

JOSEPH:

Why, Mary, that is a cherry tree;
At one time of year you might eat your fill.

MARY:

Look again, husband, more carefully;
Its blossoms are brighter than ever I saw.

JOSEPH:

Mary, come to the city speedily
Or we shall suffer the hand of the law.

MARY:

Now, my husband, look once again.

How lovely cherries cling to the tree,
And though I would not cause you pain,
I wish you would pick a few for me.

JOSEPH:

I shall try to do what you desire.—

> [*He tries awkwardly to reach a
> branch, but fails.*]

Oh, to pick these cherries I won't be beguiled.
The tree is so high and I easily tire:
Let *Him* pluck your cherries who got you with
child!

MARY:

Now, good Lord, grant this boon to me,
To have these cherries, if such is Your will.

> [*The tree bows.*]

Now I thank Thee, God; Thou hast bowed the tree
And I may gather and eat my fill.

JOSEPH:

Ah, I well know I have offended my God the Trinity
In speaking to Mary so unkind a word as this,
For now I believe it can only be
That Mary bears the Son of the King of Bliss.
May He help us in our need!
You were nobly born of Jesse's race,
Kings and prophets worthy of grace,
And you worthy of your noble place,
As learned men can read.

MARY:

Thank you, husband, for what you say
And first let us go on to our journey's end.
Almighty Father, comfort us, I pray,
And the Holy Ghost in glory be our friend.

> [*They go out.*]

SCENE V

THE ADORATION OF THE SHEPHERDS

[*The* THREE SHEPHERDS, MANFRAS, BOSERACE *and* MOIS, *lie on a hill. An* ANGEL *appears above. The manger, with* MARY, JOSEPH *and* JESUS, *on the left.*]

ANGEL:
> Joy to God Who reigns in heaven
> And peace to men on earthly ground!
> A Child is born to be your leaven;
> Through Him the folk shall be unbound.
> Sacraments there shall be seven
> Won through that Child's wound.
> Therefore I sing to Him you believe in:
> The flower of friendship now is found.
> God, who rules the earth and sea,
> Descends from heaven above to win
> Man below and heal his sin,
> Peace is come to all his kin
> Through God's subtlety.

FIRST SHEPHERD:
> Manfras, Manfras, fellow mine,
> I saw a light like silver shine,
> I never saw so strange a sign
> Shaped upon the skies.
> Brighter than the sun's beam
> On Bethlehem I saw it stream
> And over all this region gleam,
> Thrice I saw it rise.

SECOND SHEPHERD:
> You are my brother Boserace;
> I saw this miracle take place,

I know it is a sign of grace
Shining before dawn.
Balaam came to prophesy
A light should sparkle in the sky
When maid Mary's son should lie
In Bethlehem, new born.

THIRD SHEPHERD:

Though I love best silent joys,
A herdsboy whom men name as Mois,
In Moses' law I heard a voice
Calling on the cross.
Of a maid a Babe is born;
On a tree He shall be torn,
Saving folk who lie forlorn;
This Child shall heal that loss.

[*Here* THE ANGEL *sings* Gloria in excelsis.]

FIRST SHEPHERD:

Eh, eh, that was a wonderful note
Which now was sung above the sky.
I have the music all by rote.

[*Singing.*]

The song was gle, glo, glory.

SECOND SHEPHERD:

No, by my oath, it was not so.
This is the song that I would hum.
I know right well that it should go

[*Singing.*]

Gle, glo, glas, glum.

THIRD SHEPHERD:

The song, I thought, retold the story,
And afterwards I heard him say
The Child that was born shall be Prince of glory
And we should seek Him straightaway.

SECOND SHEPHERD:

> Let us follow with all our worth
> Going along with song and mirth
> To worship with joy at that blessed birth
> The Lord of all our throng.
> Let us march on speedily
> To honor that Babe worthily
> With mirth, song and melody.
>   [*They arrive at Bethlehem.*]
> Now stay and sing this song.

FIRST SHEPHERD:

> Hail, Flower of flowers, the fairest found,
> Hail, Peerless pearl, the rose we prize,
> Hail, Bloom, by whom we'll be unbound
> With Thy bloody wounds in wondrous wise.
> To love Thee is my delight!
> Hail, Flower fair and free,
> Light from the Trinity,
> Hail, blessed mayst Thou be,
>   Hail, Maiden, Mother of Might!

SECOND SHEPHERD:

> Hail, Flower over flowers the fairest to find,
> Hail, Christ, Kith and Kin of all mankind,
> Hail, Worker of weal, to mercy inclined,
> Hail, Victor of vice!
> Hail, Former and Friend,
> Hail, First to defend,
> Hail, Satan's sad end,
>   Hail, Prince of Paradise!

THIRD SHEPHERD:

> Hail, Lord over lords, who lies here low,
> Hail, King over kings, as thy kindred know,
> Hail, noblest Knight in hell's overthrow,
> Hail, Flower of all!

Hail, Worker to win
Bodies bound in sin;
Hail, in a beast's bin,
Asleep in a stall!

JOSEPH:

Herdsmen of the hill,
Be not still,
But speak your will
To many a man:
How God is born
This merry morn
To aid the forlorn
As well He can.

FIRST SHEPHERD:

We shall tell
By hill and dell
How the Harrower of hell
Was born this night,
To work well,
To crush and quell
The fiends fell
Against His right.

SECOND SHEPHERD:

Farewell, Babe and Bairn of bliss,
Farewell, Lord of lowliness,
In honor of Thee I humbly kiss
Thy feet, and freely fall.
Here I kneel upon my knee;
All the world may joy in Thee;
Now farewell, Lord of majesty,
And farewell, King of all!

THIRD SHEPHERD:

Though I am the last to take my leave
Yet, fair Infant, never grieve;
Now, fair Baby, my prayer receive;

Fair Child, now good day!
Fare Thee well, my Darling dear,
Perfect Prince without a peer,
Farewell, my Lord, and have good cheer,
Farewell, born in poor array!

MARY:

Thank you, herdsmen, heartily,
For your song and lowly bending;
My Son shall repay you royally
And give you all a right good ending.

[THE SHEPHERDS *leave*.]

SCENE VI

THE MAGI AND THE DEATH OF HEROD

[*The* THREE KINGS, BALTHAZAR, MELCHIZAR *and*
JASPER, *enter from the left following a star over Bethle-
hem, right, where* MARY, JOSEPH *and* JESUS *are seen.*
HEROD'S *palace is center.*]

FIRST KING:

Brother kings, I bid you hail,
Riding over hill and dale
To seek our Savior without fail
        Born this blessed hour.
In Saba's land I saw appear
The glad star that guides us here.
A Babe's blood shall buy us dear,
        Born in a beast's bower.

My name is king Balthazar;
Prophecies foretold this star;
And so I came from lands afar
        To seek a maiden's Son;

For He, made Man of mortal mold,
Yet is King of heaven's hold;
I will offer Him rich gold
    As reason will have done.

SECOND KING:

Melchizar my name is known,
My hot love in heart has grown
To this Blossom freshly blown
Born in a beast's bin.
In Tarsus' realm I wear the crown;
Past banks and rivers brown
I have traversed many a town
My Lord's love to win.

With frankincense I bid Him hail
Because His priesthood shall not fail,
His bright blood shall be the bail
Whereby our bond is broken.
This Child must be a chosen priest,
In Him all virtues be increased.
Incense at His Father's feast
Shall be His priestly token.

THIRD KING:

In Ipotes and Archage
I am of kingly lineage.
I seek a Child of semblance sage,
Whom I have sought afar.
Jasper the king, my name is known
In many lands I call my own;
Through bitter blasts blindly blown
I strive to seek the star.

A gift of myrrh I bring with me,
A bitter liquor verily,

For He shall suffer cruelly
When made a maiden's son;
Man and God omnipotent
Shall on a wicked tree be bent,
With bitter beating torn and rent
Till all His blood has run.

[THE KINGS *remain left.*]
[*Enter* HEROD *with* SENESCHAL *and
other followers.*]

HEROD:

Now I reign in my robes regal and rich,
Rolling in rings, in royal array:
I drive the dukes down deep in the ditch;
My doughty deeds dazzle the day!
I shall mar these men with misery,
And scorn their sacraments in fool's play.
No lords in this world are like unto me;
I will slash them and dash them to dark dismay.
I am jollier than a jay;
Breakers of law
I strike with awe
Quarter and draw,
            And hurl them away.

I am clad in a knightly kirtle today;
My countrymen know me as cruel and curst,
I sit under Caesar in sovereign sway,
I sow sorrow on scoundrels and scorn them the
    worst.
Boys boast of a bold Babe in barren abode
Born in bed with the beasts, as rumor has blown.
I shall prune that Baby and prick that Toad,
Slay Him with spear and shatter with stone!
Every man-child shall moan!

By Mahound, duke of hell,
My knights shall ride well;
Death ever befell
Him who threatened my throne.

Steward bold,
Walk on the wold,
Wisely behold
All about.
If anything
Should grieve the king
Quickly bring
The secret out.

SENESCHAL:
Lord king of crown,
I go from town
On dale and down
To bide:
Ears addrest
To east and west
Where grim guest
May hide.

[THE SENESCHAL *turns left where
he meets* THE THREE KINGS.]

Kings three,
Under this tree
In this country,
What do you do?
Herod reigns
On these plains
And here deigns
To challenge you.

FIRST KING:
Then lead us all

Whatever befall
To the king's hall;
Come, guide us on!
By the star's glow
He may show
How to know
God's noble Son.

SENESCHAL:

Follow this hour
With all your power
To the round tower
Where Herod sways:
In pomp and pride
Far and wide
Through time and tide
His rule stays.

[*The* SENESCHAL *and* THREE KINGS *enter*
HEROD'S *palace.*]

Sir King on throne,
I lead alone
Past stock and stone
These kings three.
They bear a treasure
Beyond measure,
But what is their pleasure
I cannot see.

FIRST KING:

Hail to thee, king, enthroned on high!
Hail! we greet thee, and next draw nigh!
Do you know a Child, wily and sly,
Who was born hereabouts?
He was born of a maid in virginity,
Yet the King of all kings shall be.

We go to worship His infancy
And here seek Him out.

HEROD:

You three kings, now change your tone;
Such windy words are vainly blown;
All idle nonsense lies unknown
           Unreckoned in my reign.
I am king of high degree;
No one shall be over me;
Lord of wealth by land and sea,
           And many a fertile plain.
But go and find Him now, I pray,
If such a Helper lives today;
And when upon your homeward way
           Come again to me.
I shall freely follow on
To see right honor duly done,
And worship Him as heaven's Son,
           Low on bended knee.

FIRST KING:

King, have good day!
I go my way
To find
The Lord of Might
To heal our sight
Now blind.

SECOND KING:

King full stern,
By field and fern
I go
To seek a Lord
Whose life is stored
With woe.

THIRD KING:

> If we find
> This King so kind,
> Virgin born,
> We shall come
> To your home
> Another morn.

[The KINGS *leave the castle.]*

HEROD:

> Fy, fy on the tales that I have been told
> Here before my cruel knee!
> How should a Baby grow so bold
> Born with beasts in beggary?
> He is young and I am old,
> A hardy king of high degree.
> This day the kings shall all be cold
> If they come again to me.

> *[During the following speech the* KINGS *pass
> between* HEROD'S *court and the stable in
> Bethlehem.]*

FIRST KING:

> Let us seek our Lord and Savior; the ray
> Of the star will show us His city soon;
> Save us from peril, Lord, I pray;
> And grant us to reach our joys today!
> I ask Thee for this boon.
> Hail to Thee, King meanly arrayed!
> Hail to Thee, fed with milk of a maid!
> Hail, I come with gifts, gold inlaid,
> As prophecies record;
> The richest metal of all is gold,
> Most royal and rare for men to behold;
> So gold I give Thee, and here make bold
> To acknowledge Thee my lord.

SECOND KING:

> Lord, I kneel upon my knee,
> Sweet incense I offer Thee,
> Thou shalt be first in dignity
> And none so great in might.
> In God's house, as men shall see,
> Thou shalt worship the Trinity,
> One God in persons three,
> And all one Lord of might.

THIRD KING:

> Lord, I kneel down by Thy bed,
> In Maiden's flesh incarnated,
> Known far and wide as the Godhead,
> King of all kings born.
> Bitter myrrh I bring to Thee
> For bitter blows shall ring on Thee
> And bitter death shall cling to Thee;
> On this account I mourn.

MARY:

> Kind kings, farewell!
> From fiends of hell
> God guard you well
> And be your friend
> As you homeward wend
> To your journey's end.

> > [*The* KINGS *go out right.*]

HEROD:

> I sit on my throne in midst of my host:
> This world shall bow to my majesty.
> In heaven and earth and on hell's coast
> All dread my awful dignity.
> No lord is priced at a piece of toast,
> Neither kaiser nor king, compared with me.

No beggar may brag or outblow my boast,
These rascals I'll rap, and these robbers shall flee
From my sun-bright brand!
There shall be neither kaiser nor king
Whom I shall not bring
To admit this thing
And obey my command.

My gentle knights, in duty bound,
Now in good time a feast prepare.
Let a table be royally crowned
With curious cloth and worthy fare,
Fit for the fairest prince ever found;
Of best meats and wines let no one spare.
Though a little pint cost a thousand pound!
Bring in the best food; have no care
For the cost, but see all done.

SENESCHAL:
My lord, the table duly stands,
Here is water to wash your hands.
Blow with all your might, you minstrel bands,
To bring the supper soon!

[*While trumpets blow,* DEATH, *in the form of a
skeleton entwined with worms, enters.*]

DEATH [*aside to the audience*]:
Ooooh! I heard a page praising pride
Surpassing all princes in prosperity.
He weens himself worthiest in the whole world wide;
King over all kings this lad hopes to be.
Soldiers he sent on every side
To seek Christ and kill Him cruelly.
In his wicked will the rascal lied;
God's Son still lives; there is no Lord but He,

King above all kings.
I am Death, God's messenger.
Almighty God hath sent me here
To slay this scoundrel without a tear
　　　For his wicked slaughterings.

HEROD:

Now, noble knights, be merry and glad,
And with proper service make me some mirth,
For, by my gracious Mahound, I never have had
Such joy and bliss since the time of my birth.
For my foe is dead, stricken as a toad;
No king is above me in heaven or earth;
Let joy resound through my royal abode,
Spare no meat or drink; let there be no dearth
Of wine or of bread.
King alone am I.
None so proud and high.
Knights, make a glad cry,
　　　For my foe is dead!

　　　　[*While the* KNIGHTS *shout and trumpets blare*
　　　　DEATH *suddenly seizes* HEROD *at his wine;*
　　　　SATAN *enters and takes him.*]

SATAN:

All mine! all mine! this castle is mine;
I shall drag him to my cell;
I shall teach him how to dine
And how much mirth there is in hell.
It were better to live with swine
And stink forever than there to dwell,
For in our lodging souls repine
As never human tongue can tell.
　　　Now I take my way
Bearing you forth with me

To show you our games and our glee,
How merrily live we,
Ever singing "wellaway."
[SATAN *goes off, dragging* HEROD.]

DEATH [*aside to the audience*]:
Though I am naked, in poor array,
Though worms gnaw me all about,
Look that you dread me night and day;
For all you people in this rout
Shall be as I am here today;
At Death's coming though you flout
When I challenge you as prey
You shall be mine, I make no doubt,
All naked, as you see.
Among the worms, I truly tell,
Under the earth you shall dwell;
And they shall gorge you, flesh and fell,
As they have done to me.
[*They go out.*]

SCENE VII

THE RAISING OF LAZARUS

[*The house of* LAZARUS *is on one side, a field on the other.
In the house are* LAZARUS, *his two sisters,* MARTHA *and*
MAGDALENE, *and three of their friends.*]

LAZARUS:
God, who made all things of nought
And puts them to their end again,
Save the work Thy hands have wrought,
As Thou art Lord of might and main.

O gracious God, if Thou art fain,
Comfort my sorrows speedily:
My sickness gives me so much pain
And headache, I can scarcely see.

Sister Martha and Magdalene,
Help me to bed and to undress.
I am so very sick and lean,
I never felt such great distress.
My death is come at last, I guess.
Help me to walk, and hold my head.
My heavy pain would be the less
If I were laid upon my bed.

MARTHA:
Lazarus, dear brother, have good cheer,
I hope your fever soon will slake.
Just try to sleep a little here.
You will be better when you wake.

MAGDALENE:
My gentle brother, for God's sake
Lift up your heart; you must not fall.
If you were dying, you would make
A heavy household of us all.

LAZARUS:
My wind is stopped; I cannot breathe.
I put my faith in God on high.
To Him in heaven I bequeath
My soul. Ah, sisters dear, good-bye.

[*He dies.*]

MAGDALENE:
Alas, alas, to heaven I cry!
My own dear brother here lies dead.
Our trusty friend has come to die
The last of all our kin has sped.

MARTHA:

Alas, alas, and wellaway,
Now we both are brotherless;
My heavy heart is cold as clay.
Ah, who shall aid our wretchedness?
No woman has more dolefulness.
O, sister Magdalene, what's to be done?
Who can help our heaviness
Now our brother is dead and gone?

FIRST FRIEND:

Good friends, I pray you hold your peace,
Your weeping cannot better it.
I beg you, let your sorrows cease
And help to put him in the pit.

MAGDALENE:

Alas, my heart is all unknit
When you speak so of his cold grave.
I wish some friend would kindly slit
My throat, and bury me in that cave!

SECOND FRIEND:

Head and foot are carefully wound,
The sheet is clean and fair.
Now bear him to his burial ground
And let us leave him there.

MARTHA:

That pit will fill us with despair;
But since it may no better be,
Bear the corpse into the air,
And we shall follow heavily.

[*They carry the corpse to the sepulchre.*]

THIRD FRIEND:

Bury the corpse here in this pit,
And give to God the deathless soul.

Cover the grave and fasten it,
And let no beasts tear up this hole.

MAGDALENE:

His body now has reached its goal.
My heart is murdered at the sight.
Let us sit down and make our dole,
Weeping our fill the live-long night.

[*A fourth friend enters and approaches
the group at the grave.*]

FOURTH FRIEND:

Greeting, Martha and Magdalene,
I have told Jesus what you said
About your brother's sickly mien,
How he was ill, and brought to bed.
He said this ill will soon be sped,
And bids that you shall have no fear.
He prays you to be comforted
And He Himself will soon be here.

MAGDALENE:

This prophet comes too late to save.
Our brother was buried three days before.
A great stone now covers the grave,
And stops the never-opening door.

FOURTH FRIEND:

Has Lazarus died? God took him sure!
You should not have such heaviness.
Though you should weep forevermore
It cannot help your wretchedness.

[JESUS *enters slowly;* MARTHA *rises
and approaches Him.*]

MARTHA:

Ah, gracious Lord, had You been here
My brother had been comforted;
But four days he is in the bier

And all our happiness has fled.
But now I know, though he is dead,
That whatsoever thing You crave
Of God, You gain from the Godhead;
Whatever thing You ask, You have.

JESUS:

Your brother Lazarus shall rise,
And live again as he has done.

MARTHA:

I know that at the last assize
We shall all rise to greet the sun.

JESUS:

I am that resurrection
And I am that eternal life.
The man who dies believing on
My name shall conquer death and strife.

Each man who believes in Me and is
The faithful follower of My lore
Shall conquer death; and he shall not miss
The life that lasts forevermore.
Body and soul I shall restore
To endless joy, if you believe this.

MARTHA:

My hope in Thee, O Christ, stands sure.
Thou art the Son of God in bliss.

MAGDALENE:

My sovereign Lord and Prince, I vow
Had You been here to help our own,
My brother had been with us now,
Not dead but quick, who now is gone.
But against his death no help is known—
Alas, my heart is full of woe,

To think his life so soon has flown
Whom You, Lord, also cherished so.

JESUS:

Your weeping and your words constrain
Me to weep for one so true;
I, myself, cannot restrain
But I must weep, even as you.

FIRST FRIEND:

See, this prophet weeping too.
He loved Lazarus, we are sure.
Else indeed, he would not do
As all the rest. He loved him more.

SECOND FRIEND:

A straw for that! Why should He weep?
When men are blind He gives them sight.
Might He not as safely keep
His friend by virtue of His might?

JESUS:

Where have you buried your delight?
Bring Me straightway to his grave.

MARTHA:

Lord, we easily guide You right.
He was buried in this cave.

MAGDALENE:

After we had sent our friend
He himself had not been gone
Half an hour before the end;
We buried Lazarus anon.

JESUS:

Behold the power of My Godhead!
The faithful shall witness My majesty.
Take up the stone, as I have said;
The glory of God shall shine on Me!

THIRD FRIEND:

>Our answer to Your word is swift.
>Take hold and help us, everyone—
>I pray you, sirs, help me to lift.
>I cannot raise it up alone.

FOURTH FRIEND:

>I swear this is a heavy stone,
>Hard to lift and set in fast.

FIRST FRIEND:

>Though it were twice as heavy a one,
>We four could raise it up at last.

SECOND FRIEND:

>The stone is lifted from the cave,
>And men may see a fearful sight.
>The body lies within the grave,
>Wrapped in a pitiful plight.

JESUS:

>I thank Thee, Father of main and might,
>That Thou hast heard My prayer today.
>I know full well that day or night
>Thou dost grant Me what I pray.

>But for these people hereabout
>Who doubt the power of Me and Thee,
>Bring them wholly out of doubt
>And show Our power here openly.

[*loudly*]

>Lazarus, Lazarus, dear friend to Me,
>From out thy dreary burial, come!
>By might of the High Majesty,
>Enter again thy mortal home.

LAZARUS:

>As You command I rise upright,
>Hell, heaven and earth obey Your breath,

Both God and man of greatest might,
The lock and key of life and death.

> [LAZARUS *rises from his tomb bound
> in his burial clothes.*]

JESUS:

Go to Lazarus and untie
His bands, go, break them all asunder.
Let him walk home with you on his way.
God deems this miracle no wonder.

ALL THE FRIENDS:

Thou art God, we cry all with one voice;
And, Savior, do Thee reverence.
In Thee alone our hearts rejoice,
O sovereign Lord of excellence!
Help us with grace when we go hence,
For against death no man can strive.
But death in Thee has no pretence,
And Thou mayst keep us still alive.

JESUS:

I have showed in open sight
My Godhead, clear to every eye.
I seek My passion now forthright;
The time is near when I must die.
The soul of man I now must buy;
A crown of thorns must pierce My brain;
Upon Mount Calvary on high
Upon a cross I shall be slain.

> [*They all go out.*]

ACT II

Scene I

PROLOGUE OF SATAN

[SATAN *enters clothed as a young gallant. He addresses the audience.*]

SATAN:

I am your Lord Lucifer; from hell I came;
Prince of this world and great duke of hell.
So Satan is now my rightful name.
I come to hail you, and to greet you well.
I am nourisher of sin to confusion of man;
To bring him to my dungeon to dwell in fire.
To reward my servant is my princely plan;
He shall sing my sad praises in hell's choir.
Pay good heed to your prince, my people dear;
See what sports in heaven I dared to play.
To win a thousand souls an hour is a trifle here
Since I won Adam and Eve on the first day.

But miraculous marvels move my remembrance.
Of one Christ, called Joseph and Mary's son.
Thrice I tempted Him with subtle dissemblance,
Before His forty days' fast was fully done.
He scorned to make bread of a barren stone;
Angels aided Him on the temple's spire.
His answers were more marvelous than moon or sun.
I tempted Him to vainglory, but He foiled my
    desire.

And now He has twelve disciples to attend Him,
Whom He sends as servants to each city to find

Proper provision and people to befriend Him;
His miracles amaze the people's mind.
He heals the lame, the halt, the blind;
He raised up Lazarus, who lay four days in the
    grave.
When I tempt a sinner, He comes at me from
    behind;
Magdalene He dared to pardon and to save.

He pretends to be God's Son, born of a maid,
And says that He shall die for man's salvation;
That the trial of truth shall be no more delayed
When His body and soul have separation.
But those who are under my great domination
He can never rescue and drag from woe,
If a text hold true of God's own creation,
Quia in inferno nulla est redempcio.

When the deadly day of His passion draws near
I shall rear new engines of malice and hate,
Contrive reproofs to put Him in fear
And have false witness to defame and berate.
His disciples shall leave Him in His sorry state.
A hundred wounds shall wrack Him, life and limb.
A murderous traitor shall determine His fate:
The rebukes that He gives me shall turn on Him.

See the ingenuity of my checkered disguise,
My garments fitting naturally together.
Each part correct in cut and size
From the sole of my foot to my bonnet's feather.
My long pointed shoes of the finest leather
With crimson stockings are my greatest joy;

My twenty points of lace tied with a silver tether
Make that gentleman yonder look like a boy.

I have long locks on my shoulders dangling down
To harbor live beasties that tickle men by night,
With a high bonnet for covering my crown;
I hold all beggars and poor men in despite.
In great oaths and lechery set your delight,
And maintain your estate by bribery and dinners;
If the law reprove you, say you will fight,
And gather a crowd of congenial sinners.

I have brought you new names where the old ones
     tire.
And since sin is so pleasant and each man's right,
You shall name pride honor, lust natural desire,
And covetousness wisdom, where money shines
     bright;
Wrath shall be called manhood, punishment called
     spite;
Perjury be a leader in each court or session;
Gluttony be called rest, abstinence be out of sight,
And all who preach virtue be put under repression.

The time is too short to name all my men
But all these shall inherit my eternal reign;
Though Christ may scheme, I shall put them into pen
Where they shall dwell with me forever in eternal
     pain.
Remember the mortal servants in my train;
For now I must leave you for others to play.
I shall be with you at all times when you call me
     again,
Only for a little while I go away.

Scene II

THE PASSION PLAY

*[The scene is elaborately arranged in a series of stations.
In the centre is the hill of Calvary. On the right is the
council chamber of the high priests,* CAIPHAS *and* ANNAS;
between this and Calvary is the chamber of PILATE. *On
the left is the Mount of Olives. The main actors are
always visible in their appropriate stations except when
the action requires them to pass from one to another.
When* SATAN *retires,* CAIPHAS, ANNAS, GAMALIEL,
REWFYN *and* LEON *are on the station of the high priests.*
JUDAS *leaves* JESUS *and the disciples who are at the
Mount of Olives and walks toward the high priests.*
PILATE *is on his station, attended.]*

JUDAS:

> I, Judas, have schemed a privy plan
> To make my Master's power grow cold,
> By some pretense to take this Man
> And have Him treacherously sold.
> I shall earn some Jewish gold
> And so pursue my secret way
> That nothing may be known or told
> But Jesus lost without delay.

> *[He enters the hall of the priests.]*

> Hail, priests and princes present here!
> I have happy news for you;
> For if you wish, my masters dear,
> I shall sell my Master, Christ Jesu,
> Provided His ruin shall ensue,
> As now I hold His law in scorn.
> What money shall I get to be untrue,
> And have Jesu, my Master, hung and drawn?

GAMALIEL:

> Welcome, Judas, our own dear friend,
> Lead him in, sirs, by the hand.
> We are glad to give and lend
> And always be at your command.

REWFYN:

> Judas, how much shall we pay?
> The money shall not be deferred.
> If you will give your Lord away
> You only have to say the word.

JUDAS:

> Pay me promptly what is fair
> And I shall do it, if I can.
> I have heard old men declare
> That money makes the business man.

REWFYN:

> Here are thirty pieces shining bright
> Carefully tied within a glove.
> If we may have your Lord tonight
> You shall have this and all our love.

JUDAS:

> You are good men to buy and sell;
> This bargain fills my heart with honey.
> Pay up, and I shall please you well.
> I never can say no to money.

LEON:

> Now that we have made our vow
> Friends were never glued faster.
> But, Judas, you must tell us now
> By what means to take your Master.

REWFYN:

> Many men whom we shall send
> Have never seen this Man before.

And so we all must there depend
Upon some sign to make Him sure.

LEON:

Yes, especially take care of this.
Disciples and Master are clad the same,
Some secret sign must show who is
That Man whom we must put to shame.

JUDAS:

O, as to that, friends, have no doubt;
I shall see that you shall not miss.
You must circle them about
And take the Man whom I shall kiss.
This thing is safe, you may depend.
Now I must go to my Master again.

GAMALIEL:

Farewell, Judas, our own dear friend.
We shall reward you well for your pain.
            [JUDAS *leaves the priest's court*
                        and goes off, right.]

ANNAS:

Well, sirs, we are half way through.
Jesus is ours! Now we must try
To get a keen and clever crew
Who dare to fight, and dare not fly.

GAMALIEL:

Each man take his troop aside
With torch and lantern for his light.
Be prepared by eventide
With axes, spears and broadswords bright.

CAIPHAS:

No longer let us linger then,
But let each man be fit to fight.

Secretly prepare our men;
For we must do this thing to-night.

> [*The action now commences on the
> Mount of Olives.*]

JESUS:

Dear friends and brothers, every one,
Now awake both ear and eye.
This is the time I must be gone
As holy prophets prophesy.
It is said of Me that I shall die
To save you from the devil's house,
By which ignoble torture I
Shall save the soul of man, My spouse.

Peter and your fellows, here abide
And watch till I shall come again.
I must step for prayer aside,
My flesh so quakes with fear and pain.

PETER:

Lord, at Thy bidding we remain.
Reluctantly I wait here still,
Nor go till Thou appear again
Conforming to Thy holy will.

> [JESUS *goes to one side and
> kneels in prayer.*]

JESUS:

O Father, Father, for My sake
Remove the agony from Me
Which is ordained for Me to take
To save mankind from misery—
But if it still is fit for Me
To redeem his soul from ill,

I shall not shun that destiny,
But every wish of Thine fulfill.

> [JESUS *returns to His disciples who*
> *have fallen asleep.*]

Peter, Peter, sleeping fast?
Awake your friends and sleep no more.
None of you I find aghast
At mortal pains which I endure.

> [JESUS *returns to His place to pray.*]

Father of heaven, I beg of Thee
To quiet this pain a little space,
To let me escape this agony,
As I have shunned all Sin's disgrace.
Water and blood stream down My face
From deadly pains I labor under;
My body feels My piteous case
As though its joints were torn asunder.

> [JESUS *returns to His disciples who are again*
> *sleeping. He goes back to pray a third*
> *time.*]

Father, the third time I come again.
Fulfill My errand now with speed.
Deliver Me, Father, from this pain,
And lead Me to My direst need.
O Father, give Thy Son Thy heed!
Thou knowest I lived alone for good.
It is not for Myself I bleed;
For man I shed My tears and blood.

> [*An* ANGEL *descends to* JESUS *bringing*
> *Him a chalice with the sacrament.*]

ANGEL:

Hail God and Man united here!
Thy Father asks me to present
This gift to save Thee from all fear,

And bids Thee finish His intent.
In high heaven the parliament
Has bid the soul of man be free.
From heaven to earth, Lord, Thou wast sent;
This deed belongs alone to Thee.

[*The* ANGEL *suddenly ascends.*]

JESUS:

Father, as Thou wilt shall it be,
And without Thy will nothing is.
I shall fulfill the prophecy
And die for mankind's trespasses.

[JESUS *returns to His disciples,*
who still sleep.]

Awake, Peter, you rest too long,
Rise at once without delay.
Judas, the traitor, now is strong
And comes to carry Me away.
Rise up quickly, sirs, I pray.
Open your eyes even for My sake.
Walk upon the public way,
And see them march by bush and brake.

Peter, when you see Me here forsaken
By all My friends and standing alone,
Do not grieve that I am taken
But cheer your brethren who moan.

[*While He speaks a crowd of well-armed sol-*
diers appear with fiery cressets, lanterns
and torches. JUDAS *in disguise is their*
leader.]

Sirs, you go your journey fast
To find a Man who will not flee.
Know that I am not aghast.
Tell Me whom you seek to see.

LEON:

> Whom we seek I'll tell you true:
> A traitor who must suffer death.
> We know that He is one of you;
> His name is Jesus of Nazareth.

JESUS:

> Sirs, I am here and will not flee.
> Do to Me all the harm you can.
> For, true to tell you, I am He,
> Jesus of Nazareth, the very Man.
>
> > [*All the* JEWS *fall suddenly to the earth when
> > they hear* JESUS *speak, and when He bids
> > them rise, they rise.*]
>
> Arise, sirs. Why have you fallen down?
> Is ought of your coming hither for Me?
> I stand before you all alone
> That you may feel and know and see.

REWFYN:

> Jesus of Nazareth we seek;
> We hunt the traitor eagerly.

JESUS:

> The words I spoke were clear and meek;
> I told you now that I am He.

JUDAS:

> Welcome, Jesus, my Master dear!
> I have looked for You in many a place.
> I am glad indeed to meet You here,
> I knew not where to find Your Grace.
>
> > [JUDAS *kisses* JESUS, *whereupon all the* JEWS
> > *surround* JESUS, *seize Him and with loud
> > cries drag Him about as if they were mad.*]

PETER:

> My sword is drawn. Shall I strike for Thee?—
> Answer me, Lord. Make some reply.

JESUS:

    Sheath your sword immediately.

    Who strikes with the sword by the sword shall die.

    Ah, Judas, thou art the traitor, thou!

    And thou shalt soon repent that kiss.

    Thou hadst better have been unborn; for now

    Both body and soul are lost from bliss.

GAMALIEL:

    No, Jesus, You cannot deny

    That Your treason and heresy are found.

    So study on some smart reply

    While all Your cords are closely bound.

LEON:

    Arrest this traitor and spare Him not,

    But lead him straight to Judge Caiphas—

    In many places we have sought

    To bring You there to Your disgrace.

REWFYN:

    Come on, Jesus, follow me.

    I am glad of the blows I gave You.

    You shall be hanged upon a tree

    Where a million in gold will never save You.

JESUS:

    Friends, be sure you act aright

    In binding Me with cruel bands,

    Falling on Me so at night.

    No common thief before you stands.

    Many a time with open hands

    Where the temple door unfolds

    You heard Me preach the Lord's commands

    To those who seek to save their souls.

    Why did you not arrest Me then

    Hearing Me preach and talk with you?

But now you act as raving men,
Behold, you know not what you do.

GAMALIEL:

Sirs, I command you but a word tonight,
Lead Him in haste to Caiphas.
Treat Him, too, with great despite,
And do not heed the prating ass.

[*The action shifts back to the chamber of the priests.
Meanwhile a messenger runs wildly throughout all the
audience crying again and again: "Tidings, tidings,* JESUS
OF NAZARETH *is taken!* JESUS OF NAZARETH *is taken!"
Finally he ascends the station of the high priests where
they are in session.*]

MESSENGER:

Hail, princely prelates! At your requests,
Sir Caiphas and Sir Annas, I raise my voice;
I bring you tidings to clasp to your breasts.
Jesus of Nazareth is taken! Rejoice, rejoice!

He shall be brought to you here, by his friends for-
saken.
He is coming hither with a great rout.
I was among them when He was taken,
And I tell you I nearly caught a clout.

Malchas bore a lantern and jostled their Lord.
Suddenly someone touched Him and off went his ear.
Jesus bade His disciple put up his sword,
And set Malchas' ear again, whole and clear.

By heaven, I thought it a marvellous sight!
When we first approached Him He came towards us.
He asked whom we hunted that hour of night.
Then we said we sought Jesus to come with us.

He said, "I am He; it is I whom you lack."
At that word each one of us fell on the street.
Some of us lay upon our back,
But not one was standing upon his feet.

As meek as a lamb on his feet Christ stood,
And we lay as dead, till He bade us rise.
Then we seized Him with hands all stained with
    blood,
But I felt displeased with that new guise.

Therefore take counsel, my lords, and beware,
Lest this Fellow checkmate all your plan.
By my thrift, I solemnly swear
You shall find this stranger a marvellous Man!
    [JESUS *is dragged by the soldiers into the cham-*
        ber, followed by PETER *and a crowd of men*
        and women.]

ANNAS:
    Jesus, welcome without pretence!
    We have often wished to see You in court.
    We paid Your disciple thirty pence.
    Like an ox or ass you are honestly bought.

CAIPHAS:
    Who are Your disciples who follow you about,
    And what new doctrine have you come to preach?
    Tell us something. Come, speak out
    So that what You tell others we, too, may teach.

JESUS:
    I preached openly at all hours, by moon or sun,
    In the synagogue or the temple where Jews assemble.
    Ask them what I said and what I have done.
    They can reply, and will not dissemble.

FIRST JEW:

> What, you Fellow, whom do You address?
> Do You speak to Your bishop so, You block?
> I shall slap Your saucy face, I confess,
> And give You here another knock.
>
> > [*He strikes* JESUS *on the cheek.*]

JESUS:

> If I have said amiss,
> Bear witness, all this throng.
> If I said well in this,
> He has done Me a wrong.

ANNAS TO CAIPHAS:

> Sir, prevent this wretched Man
> From ruining our holy lore.
> Bring all the witnesses you can.
> To slaughter Him therefor.

FIRST DOCTOR:

> Sir, I heard this Man maintain
> That He would lay our temple in clay,
> And then would raise it up again
> As whole as ever on the third day.

SECOND DOCTOR:

> Yes, sir, I heard Him say also
> He was God's Son, and all that—
> But many a fool imagines so;
> Yes, sir, I bet my hat!

CAIPHAS:

> What sayst Thou, Jesus? why answer not?
> Hearest Thou not what is said against Thee?
> Speak, Man, speak! speak, Thou sot!
> Hast Thou scorn to speak to me?
> Hearest Thou not how they challenge Thee?
> By sun and moon, this shall be done!
> Thou shalt tell us whether Thou art God's Son.

JESUS:

>God's Son I am. I say not nay to thee.
>And that thou shalt find at the Day of Doom
>When the Son in power and majesty
>Shall adjudge the quick and dead their home.

CAIPHAS:

>Oh, oh! alas! what words are these!
>Hear ye not how He blasphemes the Lord?
>Why need we call more witnesses?
>You all have heard His own bold word.
>Do you think Him worthy to die today?

THE CROWD:

>Yes, yes, yes, He should die; we all cry yea, yea, yea!

ANNAS:

>Take Him, beat Him and show Him no grace,
>He blasphemes God in this holy place.
>>[*The crowd beat* JESUS, *spit in His face, and pull Him about. Finally He is thrown on a stool and His face covered with a cloth.*]

FIRST JEW:

>Ah, fellows, beware what you do to this Man,
>Let Him prophesy as well as He can.

SECOND JEW:

>That shall be tried with this knotted bat.
>What ho, Jesus! who gave You that?
>>[*He hits Him.*]

THIRD JEW:

>Look out, look out! Now will I
>Learn how well He can prophesy.
>Who was that?

FIRST WOMAN:

>Why, sirs, what do you do with a wretch like this?
>Look where one of His servants is.

SECOND WOMAN:

> Ah, good man, it seems to me
> That one of His followers you should be.

PETER:

> Why, woman, I never saw that Man
> Since the world first began.

FIRST WOMAN:

> You were one of His followers here in this place.
> We can tell it by your face.

PETER:

> Woman, you are mistaken there.
> I never saw Him. I swear, I swear!

FIRST JEW:

> Ah, my friend, well met today!
> You knocked my cousin's ear away.
> When we took your Master in the yard
> Your fellows left Him without a guard.
> Now you cannot forsake Him again.
> You are from Galilee, I maintain.

PETER:

> Sir, I know Him not, by God's majesty—
> If an oath of mine will do.
> I witness to all this company
> That what I tell you now is true.

> *[A cock crows;* JESUS *looks at* PETER,
> *who weeps and goes out of the hall.]*

> Ah, why will my false heart not break my breast
> Since I left my Master so cravenly?
> Alas, where now on earth may I rest
> Till He takes me again to His company?

> When I heard the cock, He glanced at me
> As one who should say, I said this before.

Alas, I have left Him cowardly
And so I shall think forevermore.

[*He goes off.*]

CAIPHAS:

Messenger, messenger!

MESSENGER:

Here, lord, here!

CAIPHAS:

Go to Pilate, who rules us all.
Commend us to him in word and deed.
Beg him to be in the judgment hall,
We require his sovereign aid with speed.
Go in haste away.
Be sure you tarry not.

MESSENGER:

It shall be done by dawn of day.
I am as swift as thought.

[*The* MESSENGER *goes toward* PILATE'S
room and approaches PILATE.]

All hail, Sir Pilate, who reigns in majesty,
And over all Jews and their laws holds sway!
My lord bishop, Sir Caiphas, commends him to thee,
And prays thee to be in judgment at break of day.

PILATE:

Go back, my fine messenger, commend me, too.
I shall come in haste, and so you may say
At the hour of nine I shall follow you
And be at the council without delay.

[*The* MESSENGER *returns to the priests.*]

MESSENGER:

Hail, my lords and bishops and princes of the law.
Sir Pilate commends him to you, and bids me say
He will come at daybreak in state and awe
And be there at prime without delay.

CAIPHAS:

Well may you fare, my gentle page;
Take this gift for your embassage.

[JUDAS *enters.*]

JUDAS:

I, Judas, have sinned and committed treason,
For I have betrayed His innocent blood.
Here is all your money I took without reason.
I am mad with grief at my hardihood.

ANNAS:

What is this to us here now?
This bargain was your own device.
You sold Him as a horse or cow
And you yourself must pay the price.

[JUDAS *throws down the money, goes
out and hangs himself.*]

CAIPHAS:

Sirs, the night has passed, the day is come
And Pilate bides in the hall alone;
It is time this Man knew His doom
And that we should bring Him to Pilate's throne.
Then let no negligence be found.

FIRST JEW:

Yes, lord, your word is quickly done.

SECOND JEW:

Yes, but see Him thoroughly bound.

THIRD JEW:

He is safe enough. Now hurry on.

[*They lead* JESUS *about the stage till
they come to* PILATE'S *station.*]

CAIPHAS:

Sir Pilate, hear our humble cause.
We have brought Jesus here for blame.
He would destroy our holy laws
And bring us all to bitter shame.

FIRST DOCTOR:

Yes, sir, but His worst is to abuse
Caesar, our lord, and leave us dowerless.
He calls Himself the King of the Jews
As though our Emperor were powerless!

PILATE:

What do you say, Man, in your cause?
Can You prove Yourself abused?
The people claim You bring them laws
That in our days were never used.

JESUS:

Their accusations hurt Me not,
Unless they hurt themselves or others so.
I have not found the thing I sought.
My Father's will now bids Me go.

PILATE:

By this then I judge You are King of kings,
God's Son and Lord of all below,
Lord of this earth and of all things.
Tell Me the truth if this be so.

JESUS:

All who hear Me and believe
Keeping their purpose steadfastly,
Though they were dead, I shall receive
Into the bliss of eternity.

PILATE:

I find no fault in Him at all,
No treason, crime or any guilt.
Justice herself would therefore fall
If His own faultless blood were spilt.

ANNAS:

Sir, in a word, our justice bleeds.
We took Him for His wicked deeds.
If Jesus had not been untrue,
We had not brought Him here to you.

PILATE:

Take Him, then, to serve your cause
And judge Him after your own laws.

CAIPHAS:

It is not lawful, you maintain,
That Jewish courts should have men slain.
So rather than have this Man our King
We pray you for His slaughtering.
Kings, my lord, we will have none
Except our Emperor alone.

PILATE:

Jesus, are You King of Jewry?

JESUS:

You have said as much to Me.

PILATE:

Then make plain
Where you reign.

JESUS:

I answer in a single word,
My kingdom is not of this world.
If My kingdom had been here
No judge had forced Me to appear.

PILATE:

Sirs, advise you as you can,
I find no fault in yonder Man.

ANNAS:

Take heed, sir, of our thorough view
And knowledge of this dangerous Man.
It is not for a day or two
But many years since He began—
You know when and where He hatched His plan,
How many thousands heard His plea,
And how His subtle treason ran
From here as far as Galilee.

PILATE:

    Sirs, since you all will have it so
    And none of you has any heart,
    Prepare to put Him to his woe
    While I examine Him apart.

                      [PILATE *takes* JESUS *to one side.*]

PILATE:

    Jesus, what say You? Here You see
    How all these Jews will force my hand.
    You might remain at peace with me
    But for the people of Your land.

JESUS:

    Thou hast no power at all on Me,
    Except My Father give it thee.
    Doing My Father's will I come
    To save Mankind from Satan's doom.
    He who betrays Me at this hour
    Comes more than thou in Satan's power.

FIRST DOCTOR:

    Princes and lords, just look and see
    How Pilate leans to Jesus' side,
    Damning our laws irreparably,
    And even damning us beside.

                    [PILATE *leaves* JESUS *and returns to the* JEWS.]

PILATE:

    Sirs, what will you have me do?
    Nothing I find in Him but good.
    Let Him free, I counsel you,
    And spare to spill His guiltless blood.

CAIPHAS:

    Pilate, I say you do a wrong
    Against our law by words like these.

The people's voice is loud and strong,
And loud their lawful witnesses.

ANNAS:

Yes, and if He escape this time,
All of us will see to this:
You will answer for His crime
And Caesar learn of your amiss!

PILATE:

Well then, since you still reply
That at all costs Jesus must die,
Artis, bring water here to me
And my doing all shall see.

> [*The servant* ARTIS *brings* PILATE
> *a basin and water.*]

As I wash my hands with water
I am guiltless of His slaughter.

FIRST DOCTOR:

The blood of Christ be upon us
And all our children after us!

> [*The crowd shouts, Yes, yes, yes!* PILATE *then
> leads* JESUS *out once more before them.*]

PILATE:

Take Him, sirs, and lead Him hence,
For I find in Him no offense.

SECOND DOCTOR:

Deliver Him, deliver Him! He is at loss
And we shall fix him to His cross.

PILATE:

Sirs, would you crucify your King?

THIRD DOCTOR:

Sir, Caesar is our only king.

PILATE:

Then since it must needs be so
To the judgment we must go.

Let the criminals appear
To receive their judgment here.

> [PILATE *takes his seat. The officers lead to the bar first* BARRABAS, *then the two thieves and* JESUS. ANNAS *and* CAIPHAS *stand beside* PILATE.]

Barrabas, hold up your hand,
Let all the people see you stand.—
Sirs, what of this thief and traitor bold?
Shall he go free, or be kept in hold?

FIRST DOCTOR:

In honor of our Paschal Day
Let this man go free away.

PILATE:

Then, Barrabas, I pardon thee,
And give a license to go free.

> [BARRABAS *goes out.*]

Dysmas and Jesmas, the court demands
That each of you hold up your hands.
Sirs, what say you of these twain?

SECOND DOCTOR:

That they are guilty and should be slain!

PILATE:

What say you of Jesus of Nazareth?

FIRST DOCTOR:

Sir, He shall be put to death!

PILATE:

So you say, but for what cause?

SECOND DOCTOR:

Sir, we all wish Him on the cross.

> [*The crowd shouts in a great voice, yes, yes, yes!*]

PILATE:

Jesus, your people have disapproved
All that for You I've said and moved.—

I charge you all to swear one thing,
Or to withstand my wrath and scorn:
Let no man dare to touch your King
Unless a knight, or gently born.
First, take His cloak and garments off,
And bare Him to His misery,
Bind Him to a pillar, and scoff
And scourge Him with whips for all to see.
When He is beaten, crown Him King
And take Him to Calvary, suffering.
Hang Him by three nails to the cross,
And let Him there bewail His loss.
Put a nail through either hand,
To left and right, as I command.
Smite the third through both His feet,
A long, sharp nail, thereunto meet.
But yet He shall not hang alone;
On either side there shall be one.
Dysmas, now I sentence thee:
Hang upon the right hand tree.
Jesmas shall hang on the left hand tree,
On Calvary for all to see.

> [PILATE *leaves his seat and retires to the back-*
> *ground accompanied by the bishops. The*
> JEWS *shout aloud, pull off* CHRIST'S *clothes,*
> *bind Him to a pillar and scourge Him.*]

THE CROWD:

Be glad, our King,
At Your triumphing!

> [*After the scourging they put a robe of purple*
> *silk upon Him, place Him on a stool and*
> *thrust a crown of thorns on His head. The*
> JEWS *kneel to* CHRIST. *They put a scepter*
> *in His hand and mock Him. Then they pull*

off the purple robe, dress Him again in his
own clothes, place the cross on His neck
and drag Him with ropes towards Calvary.
WOMEN *meet Him, weeping and wringing*
their hands.]

FIRST WOMAN:

Ah, Jesus, Jesus, woe is me!
Thou art despoiled and put to shame.
And yet no fault was found in Thee,
And Thou ever hadst a gracious name.

SECOND WOMAN:

Alas, good Jesus, this is sad
That Thou shouldst die against the right.—
Ah, wicked men, you are more than mad
To do the Lord so great despite!

JESUS:

Daughters of Jerusalem, weep not for Me,
But weep for yourselves and your children so.
For the days draw near, as all shall see,
When their sin and blindness shall turn to woe.

To the hills and the mountains they shall cry and
call,
Open and hide us from God on His throne!
Or else cover us wholly by Your fearful fall
That we may hide in your shade, and weep alone.

[JESUS *turns away from* THE WOMEN. SIMON
enters just as JESUS *has stumbled and*
fallen.]

FIRST JEW:

Sir, if you will be so good,
Here a Man is passing by
Bearing a cross of heavy wood
Whereon He must be hung on high.

So we pray you urgently
To take the cross which Jesus bore,
And bear it on to Calvary,
Earning our honest thanks therefor.

SIMON:

I have an errand, as you see,
And cannot stop to help you so.
Truly, I beg you, pardon me;
Good sirs, I pray you, let me go!

SECOND JEW:

What, you rascal, do you scorn
To do our bidding, and bear this bar?
You shall, however you are sworn,
Though it were twenty times as far!

SIMON:

O peace, sirs, you misjudge my thought.
I will bear it patiently
Wherever you will have it brought,
Just as you have commanded me.

    [SIMON *takes the cross from* JESUS *and they
proceed once more.* VERONICA *enters.*]

VERONICA:

Ah, sinful people, what do you do?
He sweats and bleeds and cannot see.—
O gentle Prophet, good and true,
I am sad at heart for Thee.

    [*She wipes His face with
her handkerchief.*]

JESUS:

Veronica, now I suffer less.
My face is clean, as all may see.
I shall keep all men from distress
Who look on her kerchief and think of Me.

    [*The procession reaches Calvary. They
pull off* CHRIST'S *clothes.*]

FIRST JEW:

Come on now, and let us try
How the limbs and wood shall meet.
Cast Him down to earth, say I!
How long will He stand upon His feet?

> [*Having fastened* CHRIST *to the cross,
> they dance about Him.*]

SECOND JEW:

Look, friend, there he lies, tacked on a tree!

THIRD JEW:

Ah, yes indeed, you're a royal king!

FOURTH JEW:

Good sir, what about your prophecy?

FIRST JEW:

Or what of that false, vile arguing?

SECOND JEW:

Sirs, set the cross on high
That all may see His face.

THIRD JEW:

Kneel to our king and cry
For mercy and for grace!

> [*They erect the cross.*]

FOURTH JEW:

Hail, King, if so You be.

FIRST JEW:

Yes, there You hang in open view.

SECOND JEW:

Come from off the tree.

THIRD JEW:

Then all will worship You.

> [*The poor common people look disapprovingly
> at the Jewish soldiers, who in turn force four
> or five of them to aid in hanging the two
> thieves.*]

FOURTH JEW:

Come, knaves, set these two crosses right
And hang these two as we command.

FIRST JEW:

Then to serve this worthy knight
Put the two on either hand.

> [*The two thieves are hung on their crosses. The*
> FOUR JEWS *quarrel over the dice as they*
> *play for* CHRIST'S *clothes. Meanwhile there*
> *enter before the cross of* CHRIST THE
> VIRGIN MARY, MARY MAGDALENE, MARY
> SALOME, MARY JACOBI, *and* SAINT JOHN.]

THE VIRGIN:

Ah, my good Lord and darling Child,
What have You done to hang so high?
Was there no other death more mild
But the shameful death which thieves must die?

JESUS:

O Father Almighty, Maker of man,
Forgive these Jews who pierced Me through.
Pardon them, Father, as You can,
For they know not what they do.

FIRST JEW:

So ho, so ho! now here is He
Who would do our temple quite away,
And then by sleight and sorcery
Raise it whole on the third day.

SECOND JEW:

Now if You can do such a deed,
Help yourself as best You can.
Then we shall believe in You, indeed,
And say You are a mighty man.

THIRD JEW:

If You are God's Son, as you teach,
Quickly from the cross come down;

Then we surely shall beseech
Your grace, and grant you great renown!

JESMAS [*on the left*]:
If You are God's Son, as You say,
Why should we all three suffer thus?
I find my own faith turn away
For the Son of God would succour us.

DYSMAS [*on the right*]:
Be still, you fool, and stop your din.
He is God's Son as the Scripture saith.
All His life long He did no sin
For which He should endure this death.
While both of us are justly caught
He never did a thing amiss.
Help me, Lord, help me! Forget me not
When you come as King to Your kingdom of bliss.

JESUS:
Amen, amen, your words are wise.
Gladly will I grant your prayer.
You shall be with Me in paradise;
This day Your God will greet you there.

THE VIRGIN:
O my Son, my Darling, my Dear,
How have I offended Thee
That Thou shouldst speak to all these here
And not a word at all to me?
You are gentle to the Jews
And have forgiven all their crimes.
Even the thief receives glad news
And gets the meed of heaven betimes.

JESUS:
Ah woman, woman, behold thy son,
And thou, John, behold thy mother!
I lay this precious charge upon
One chaste maid to keep another.

Woman, My Father in heaven sent
Me to thee to put Adam's fine away;
It is My Father's high intent
That My death should deliver the devil's prey.
Since My Father wills all this to be
Your grief for Me is wrongly forced.
To die for man was I born of thee,
To give to man the bliss he lost.

[THE VIRGIN *embraces the cross.*]

MAGDALENE:

Ah, good lady, what do you do?
Your tears and cries augment our sore.
When Jesus sees such grief in you
It makes His misery the more.

THE VIRGIN:

I pray you all to leave me here
And hang me up upon this tree
Beside my Son and Friend so dear,
For where He is, I too would be.

JOHN:

Leave these cries as too disheartening,
Do, gentle lady, as we do, I pray.
Comfort Our Lord at His departing
For He has almost passed away.

[JOHN *leads* MARY *from the cross to one side.*
PILATE *and* CAIPHAS, ANNAS *and their at-
tendants leave their hall and come to look
at* CHRIST.]

CAIPHAS:

Look, sirs, look, behold and see
Where He hangs who once helped many a man.
If You are God's Son verily
Come, help Yourself here,—if You can.

ANNAS:

> Yes, if You are King of Israel,
> Come down from the cross among us all.
> And if Your God can guard You well,
> We shall crown You our King imperial!
>
> > [PILATE *requests pen and ink and a tablet on
> > which he writes. He then fixes the inscrip-
> > tion to the cross which reads: "This is Jesus
> > of Nazareth, King of the Jews."*]

CAIPHAS:

> Sir Pilate, we wonder that you use
> To write Him here the King of Jews.
> We would have you change this thing
> To read, "He calls Himself their king."

PILATE:

> What I have written, written is,
> And I will have it only this.
>
> > [PILATE *and the priests return to
> > their council chamber.*]

JESUS:

> Eloy, eloy,
> > Lamabathany!
> Ah, My Heavenly Father on high,
> > Why dost Thou forsake me?
> The weakness of My human kind
> Makes My pain to shoot and grind.
> Ah, dear Father, hold Me in mind,
> > Give Me death to slake Me!

SECOND JEW:

> He called Elias, it seemed to me.
> Let us look nearer now, to see
> Whether the prophet comes privily
> > To the rescue of his highness.

JESUS:

>No man has had so keen a thirst
>As I to rescue man accurst.
>My parching lips are almost burst
>>Asunder by their dryness.

THIRD JEW:

>I shall slake that thirst, sir knave.
>Gall and vinegar I have.
>>[*He lifts the drink on a sponge.*]
>What! You look a little grave.
>>Isn't this good drink?
>You bawled aloud for drink in haste,
>But all my labor flows to waste.
>Perhaps it has too sour a taste,
>>Tell me what You think!

FOURTH JEW:

>Aloft, sir Rascal, You are set,
>And though we cannot linger, yet
>Before we go a grimace let
>>Us make and many a mow.
>We greet You well with mock and scorn,
>And pray You, both at even and morn,
>To keep a sharp eye on our corn
>>And frighten off the crow.

JESUS:

>*In manus tuas, Domine.*
>Father in heaven eternally,
>I offer up My soul to Thee,
>>Mine end has come at last.
>I shall slay Satan on hell's floor.
>I hear My heart crack at the core.
>I shall speak as man no more.
>>*Nunc consummatum est.*

>>>>>>[*He dies.*]

THE VIRGIN:

> I live too long; my heart is stung
> To see my sweet Son so upstrung
> Where the common thieves are hung,
>> Yet He unjustly curst.
> My darling Child, my Son, must die.
> Now my sorrow mounts on high
> And all my joy is passing by.
>> I believe my breast will burst.

JOHN:

> Blessed Lady, hear me well.
> Had He not died, we all should dwell
> Forever with the fiends of hell
>> In pains that ever smart.
> He suffered death for our own sin
> That so mankind may enter in
> To heavenly joys that now begin.
>> Therefore be glad in heart.
>> [*While* CHRIST'S BODY *is still hanging on the
>> cross, the* SOUL OF CHRIST *passes through
>> the entire audience, then approaches the
>> mouth of hell, extreme right, and speaks.*]

SOUL OF CHRIST:

> Now all mankind in heart be glad,
> With all the mirth that may be had.
> The soul of man will soon be bade
>> To leave the pit of hell.
> From death to life I quickly rise,
> From pain to bliss in Paradise,
> Therefore man too shall arise
>> And live in bliss as well.

> I am the Soul of Christ Jesu,
> As King of kings I come to you.

My body is dead. The Jews slew
    That body on the rood.
Rent, and torn and bloody red
For man's sake My body is dead,
For man's help My body is bread,
    And soul's drink, My body's blood.

Though My body now is slain,
The third day begins My reign
For I shall raise My body again
    To living life and praise.
Now will I go straight to hell
To fetch from fiends the souls that fell;
And all My friends who therein dwell
    Shall live in bliss always.

> [THE SOUL *goes to the gates of hell, and shouts:*
> *"Attollite portas principes vestras et eleva-*
> *mini portae eternales et introibit rex*
> *gloriae"* . . .]

Undo your gates of sorcery.
On man's soul I have memory.
Here comes your King in majesty
    To break and burst hell-hold.
You devils who are there within,
The gates of hell you must unpin;
I Myself shall save man's kin
    With vengeance manifold.

BELIAL:
    Alas, alas, ow, ow, ow, ow!
    Unto Thy bidding we must bow,
    Thou art God; we know it now,
        You filled us all with fear.

Against Thy will no strength may stand.
All things obey Thy mighty hand,
Heaven and hell, water and land,
    All serve Thee, far or near.

SOUL OF CHRIST
    Time of mercy now is past;
    No strength may hold your fortress fast.
    Hell's halls fall at last
        Before the King of glory.

Your dark door I dash down,
My fair friends I now crown,
And bring them to My royal town
    Out of their Purgatory.

    [*At these words the bars fall back from
    hell-mouth, the devils rush back, and* THE
    SOUL OF CHRIST *disappears, pursuing their
    flight.*]

CENTURION [*surveying the cross*]:
    Now I know by clearest sight
    That God's dear Son is nailed on a tree.
    Wondrous signs confirm His right:
    Quod vere filius dei erat iste.

FIRST JEW:
    The very child of God is He,
    As we by many marvels mark:
    Earth quakes; its trembling troubles me;
    The mist and storm grow wondrous dark.

SECOND JEW:
    Jesus is sure, by your leave.
    We need not break a bone.
    He is dead, I believe.
    He will not move or moan.

FIRST JEW:

> Let us make sure that this is so;
> I have plans to prove us right.
> Wait here a moment while I go
> To fetch to us that blinded knight.
>
> > [*He goes to meet* LONGEUS *who
> > approaches from left.*]
>
> Greetings, good sir Longeus.
> I pray you now right heartily
> That you will go at once with us.
> It is for your honor certainly.

LONGEUS:

> At your request I go with you
> Into whatever place you will.
> I believe you are my friend, and true.
> Lead on, and God be with us still.

FIRST JEW:

> Sir Longeus, take in hand this spear,
> Long and sharp and clean of rust.
> Heave it up and hold it here.
> There is your game. Now thrust, man, thrust.
>
> > [LONGEUS *lifts the spear warily, but pierces*
> > CHRIST'S *body. The blood flowing down the
> > spear wets his hand. With his hand he rubs
> > his eyes, and regains his sight.*]

LONGEUS:

> Ah, good Lord, how can this be
> That I can now see all things bright?
> Thirty winters I could not see,
> And now by miracle all is light.
> Who is He who hangs upright?
> I believe He is the Virgin's Son.
> That this is true I know aright,
> For this the cruel Jews have done.
>
> > [*He kneels.*]

Now God forgive me that
Which I have done to Thee!
I did I knew not what.
The Jews betrayed even me.
   Have mercy, have mercy, have mercy!
  [JOSEPH of *Arimathea and* NICODEMUS *come*
   to Calvary. JOSEPH, *aided by* NICODEMUS,
   sets up ladders beside the cross.]

NICODEMUS:
Joseph of Arimathea, blessed art thou
Because thou dost a gentle deed.
I pray thee, let me help thee now
That I may share thy righteous meed.

JOSEPH:
Nicodemus, welcome indeed!
I rather beg for help from you.
He will give to each his meed.
And I have leave for what I do.
  [MARY *and* JOHN *now come forward.* JOSEPH
  climbs a ladder on one side, NICODEMUS *on*
  the other. They take the body down and
  lay the head in MARY'S *lap.*]
See, Mary mother good and true,
Your bleeding Son, pale with His woes,
He tears my heavy heart in two,
Kiss Him once before He goes.

THE VIRGIN:
Ah mercy, mercy my Son so dear!
Thy bleeding face I now must kiss.
Thy face is pale and void of cheer.
All my joys I too shall miss.
No mother saw such scenes as this,
Or saw her son so spoiled by woe.
My dear Child never did amiss!
Merciful Father of Heaven, why should it be so?

JOSEPH:

> Mary, give your Child to me.
> Please now, let me bury your Son.

THE VIRGIN:

> Joseph, blessed may you be
> For the kind deed that you have done.

> *[They go to the sepulchre and*
> *lay the body in it.]*

JOSEPH:

> I give Thee linen I have bought
> To wind Thee in while it is new.

NICODEMUS:

> Here is an ointment that I have brought
> To anoint the limbs of Lord Jesu.

JOSEPH:

> Now Jesus lies within his grave
> Which sometime was ordained for me.
> This gift, my Lord, I gladly gave
> Knowing my thanks should come from Thee.

NICODEMUS:

> Now let us close the stone again
> And lay Our Lord at length to rest.
> Let us walk home across the plain,
> The day is sinking in the west.
> Farewell, Joseph, kind and true,
> We cannot tarry more than this.

JOSEPH:

> Sir, God Almighty be with you
> And take you to eternal bliss.

THE VIRGIN:

> Fare you well, my princely friends,
> In joy and gladness may you be.
> The bliss of heaven that never ends
> Shall gladden you eternally.

[JOSEPH *and* NICODEMUS *bow to* THE VIRGIN
*and depart, leaving her at the sepulchre. She
shortly takes up her station at a shrine
known as The Temple. The action is now
resumed on* PILATE'S *station. He is attended
by* ANNAS, CAIPHAS *and four soldiers*,
ARPHAXAT, AMOURANT, COSDRAM *and*
AFFRAUNT.]

CAIPHAS:

Listen, Pilate, to what I shall say.
I have sour and tart advice.
We must guard ourselves straightway,
Or we may later pay the price.
You know, my lord, that Christ Jesu
Made a mighty matter plain,
Boasting the thing which He would do:
The third day He would rise again.
If those disciples who remain
Steal the buried corpse away,
They will assuredly maintain
That He arose on the third day.
So to still these proud alarms
Take stalwart men and bind them fast
To watch the grave with force of arms
Till the third day is fully past.

PILATE:

Step out there, Sir Amouraunt,
And Sir Arphaxat, do you so.
Sir Cosdram and Sir Affraunt,
Save our state from overthrow.
Sirs, to Jesus you shall go
And watch till three long days have flown.
See that neither friend nor foe
In any manner touch the stone.

If His disciples reappear
To fetch the body thus away,
Knock them down; and have no fear
If you should make their lives your prey.
By your gods and by your lives,
Never let the rascals hence;
So your children and your wives
Should perish for your negligence.

ARPHAXAT:

No, my lord, we truly swear
They shall not escape us now.

AMOURAUNT:

Though a hundred fought us there,
They should die, I make a vow.

COSDRAM:

A hundred, fie; three hundred sure
Would not be able to withstand,—

AFFRAUNT:

Yes, if a hundred thousand more
Should come, I'd kill them with my hand.

PILATE:

Well, sirs, then do your part
And, look you, take good heed.
Without more words, depart
And let the watch proceed.
Now, Sir Caiphas, what can you say?
Is not this matter settled here?

CAIPHAS:

Our danger, sir, is done away,
And we are free from any fear.

[*The knights arrive at the sepulchre.*]

ARPHAXAT:

Look, sir Amouraunt, where will you be?
Will you take the feet or head?

AMOURAUNT:
>   I take the head, most certainly.
>   Whoever comes this way is dead.

ARPHAXAT:
>   And I will by the feet abide
>   Though Jack should come and Jill.

COSDRAM:
>   I will guard the right-hand side.
>   Whoever comes this way, I kill.

AFFRAUNT:
>   I will keep the other hand.
>   Whatever traitor dare withstand
>   Shall perish at my lord's command
>   >   And by my deadly blows.
>   Sir Pilate now may take good cheer,
>   For we shall guard the body here,
>   Standing watch about the bier,
>   >   Whoever comes or goes.

PILATE:
>   Now, gentle followers, every one,
>   Come with me to seal the stone
>   That Jesus rise not to His throne
>   >   Now that He is dead.

CAIPHAS:
>   We grant it well, and we shall go.
>   When it is sealed and guarded so
>   He can strike no second blow,
>   >   And we need have no dread.
>   >   >   [PILATE *and his companions go*
>   >   >   *to the sepulchre.*]

ANNAS:
>   Here is wax prepared and pure;
>   Set on your seal that shall endure.
>   Then, I say, you may be sure
>   >   He shall not rise or stir.

PILATE:

This corner is mine: I fasten it.
He shall never leave this pit.
I swear that He shall never flit
    Out of this sepulchre.

ANNAS:

Here is further wax for you.
These sealings all must stay.
And when a lock is added too,
    We shall go our way.
Leave these knights to guard the tomb,
And if his followers slyly come
To take their Master's body home
    They'll bring them to us without delay.

PILATE:

Armoured knights,
Like storm-sprites,
Guard our rights,
Be brave and leal;
Be you bold
To keep this hold,
And you will have gold
And helms of steel.

            [PILATE *and the priests return*
                      to their chamber.]

AFFRAUNT:

Now in this ground
He lies bound
Who suffered wound
For false was He.
The left part here
I keep from fear,
Armed clear
From head to knee.

COSDRAM:

> I will have this side
> Whatever betide.
> If any man ride
> To steal the corse,
> I'll see him plied
> With wounds wide.
> My glaive shall glide
> With fine force.

AMOURAUNT:

> The head I take
> And here I wake,
> A steel stake
> I hold in hand.
> Crowds quake,
> Crowns break,
> Shafts shake,
> But I stand.

ARPHAXAT:

> Armed complete
> I guard the feet.
> A bloody sheet
> Wraps them about.
> If mad men stalk
> By brook or balk
> Their tall talk
> I put to rout.

AFFRAUNT:

> My heart palls,
> My head falls
> Asleep.
> This burial ground
> Hell's hound
> Must keep.

COSDRAM:

> I say the same.
> I fear no blame,
> But fall.
> Mahound, thou whelp,
> After thy help
> I call!

AMOURAUNT:

> I am heavy as lead.
> Despite my dread,
> I sleep.
> This stone tonight
> Mahound's might
> Must keep.

ARPHAXAT:

> I am not strong
> To stand so long,
> But sink.
> I drop this task;
> I only ask
> A wink.

> > [*The* FOUR SOLDIERS *fall asleep.* THE SOUL OF
> > CHRIST *now returns through hell-mouth,
> > leading forth* ADAM, EVE, ABRAHAM, JOHN
> > THE BAPTIST *and others.*]

SOUL OF CHRIST:

> Come forth, Adam and Eve, with Me
> And all My friends who herein be,
> To Paradise come forth with Me,
> > And dwell in endless bliss.
> The fiend of hell who was your foe
> Shall now be wrapped and wrung in woe;
> From woe to welfare we must go,
> > No joy so great as this.

ADAM:

> I thank Thee, Lord, to so erase
> My sin and show Thy greater grace!
> Now we shall win a blissful place
>> In joy and endless mirth.
> Man was through my sin forlorn;
> To save man the flesh was torn
> That once in Bethlehem was born,
>> And blessed be Thy birth!

EVE:

> Blessed be Thou, Lord of life!
> I am Eve, Adam's wife.
> Thou hast suffered sorrow and strife
>> For works that we have wrought.
> Thy mild mercy has all forgiven.
> Death's dints on Thee were driven.
> Now we shall live with Thee in heaven,
>> By Thy bright blood bought.

JOHN THE BAPTIST:

> I am Thy cousin, John, thine own.
> Thy wounds are beaten to the bone.
> Where Jordan's banks were overflown
>> I hastened to baptize.
> Through the deed that Thou hast done
> We escape from Satan, every one,
> And go in glee and gladness on
>> To bliss in Paradise.

ABRAHAM:

> I am Abraham, who abode
> After Noah's deluge flowed.
> A sorry sin Adam sowed
>> That clad us all in care.
> A Son who sucked a maiden's breast
> Has bled his blood to make us blest,

And bought us back from hell's arrest;
    From foe to friend we fare.

SOUL OF CHRIST:
Fair friends whom I have won,
On you in sooth shines the sun,
The devil's days are dark and done
    For I shall fetter him fast.

[*to* SATAN]:
As a wicked worm you dared appear
To tempt and try my children dear.
Therefore, traitor, tremble here
    And come to grief at last.

SATAN:
Howl! Howl! I now am bound!
In hell's hole my home is found,
In wild woe wrapt around
    In devil's den I dwell.
In hell's lodge I lie alone;
With grizzly grief I growl and groan,
The fiends are false; my friends are flown;
    And I shall never come from hell.

SOUL OF CHRIST:
Now your foe is bound in hell
Who sought you out to crush and quell.
And I shall rise, though flesh and fell
    Were rent for your dear sake.
My body hangs upon the rood.
And though the Jews were rough and rude,
It shall rise to be your food,
    And flesh and blood awake.
        [THE SOUL OF CHRIST *enters the sepulchre.* THE
        RISEN CHRIST *emerges from the tomb and
        addresses the audience.*]

By hard ways I have gone,
And suffered pain in flesh and bone,
Stumbling still by stock and stone.
  For three and thirty years.

I lighted from my Father's throne.
To make amends for man's moan.
My flesh was flayed, man, for thine own.
  The blood I bled appears.

For man's love, I God, was dead;
For man's love I rise all red;
For man I have made My body bread,
  Man's soul to feed.

Man, if thou now wilt have Me gone,
And will not follow Me alone,
No friends or followers of Thine own
  Will help Thee in Thy need.

   [JESUS *goes to the temple on the left*
    where MARY *is kneeling.*]

Salve, Sancta parens, My mother dear,
Hail to Thee, mother, and happy cheer!
Now is risen with body clear
  Thy Son once delved deep.

Now is the day, as I foretold,
When I should rise, though clay is cold.
Behold Me here from hell's hold.
  Therefore cease to weep.

THE VIRGIN:
 Welcome, my Lord, before my face!
 Welcome, my Son, my Help, my Grace!
 I shall worship Thee in every place.
  Welcome, Lord God of might.

A great sorrow in heart had I
To see Thee suffer, bleed and die.
Now my joy is raised on high.
    All men shall hail this sight.

JESUS:

All this world, once forlorn,
Shall worship thee at eve and morn,
For if of thee I had not been born,
    Man had been lost in hell.
I was dead, but life I gave,
Though I died, I died to save.
Now that I rise from out the grave
    Man shall rise as well.

THE VIRGIN:

Ah, dear Son, your words are good!
You have stilled my weeping mood.
Blessed be the precious blood
    That you so gladly gave!

JESUS:

Dear Mother, now I go My way.
Be ye gleeful, glad and gay.
Death dies and Life wakes today.
    I am arisen from My grave.

                              [*He goes out.*]

    [THE VIRGIN *resumes her silent prayer.* THE
    SOLDIERS *about the sepulchre now awake in
    terror as though they had seen hell in their
    sleep.*]

AMOURAUNT:

Awake, awake!
The hills quake,
The trees shake
And fall asunder.

Gashes given,
Darts driven,
Ears riven
As by thunder.

ARPHAXAT:
Christ is risen, none can say nay,
Though He is dead and cold in clay.
Faith too is arisen today.
          I am struck with wonder.
He has risen by His own might,
And gone upon His way forthright.—
How shall we soldiers stand the spite
          Pilate must labor under?

COSDRAM:
Let us go
To tell this woe,
Reporting so
And make all plain.
Truth to say,
Out of clay
He rose today
        Whom Jews had slain.
              [*The* FOUR SOLDIERS *hasten out.*]

SCENE III

THE APPEARANCE TO MAGDALENE

[MARY MAGDALENE *is seen mourning beside the empty sepulchre.*]

MAGDALENE:
My heart breaks, my soul is ill,
Streaming tears wash my face.

Sorrow makes me sad and still,
My gracious Lord has left the place.
Mine own dear Lord and King of grace
Drove seven devils from my womb.
Now this has been His last disgrace
That He is stolen from the tomb.

ANGEL [*entering*]:

Woman, why stand you here alone?
Why do you mourn and weep so sore?
What cause have you to make your moan?
What is your bitter sorrow for?

MAGDALENE:

I have cause to weep forevermore,
My Lord's body has left this pit.
Men have taken His body away
And I know not what they have done with it.

> [THE ANGEL *goes out.* MAGDALENE
> *walks about the sepulchre.*]

Alas, alas for all my woe!
My Lord has gone and passed me by.
Where can I go? What can I do?
My joy has flown; my heart is dry.

> [JESUS, *dressed as a gardener, ap-
> proaches and stands behind her.*]

JESUS:

Woman, why do you weep and sigh?
Tell me what troubles you have had.
Why do you shiver so and cry?
Why do you sob and seem so sad?

MAGDALENE:

No woman had a better cause
To weep and wail by night and day
Than I myself, who cannot pause
In heavy sorrow ever and aye.

Alas from pain my heart bleeds blood.
My Lord is taken far away.
I must moan in mournful mood
For where He is, I cannot say.
But, gentle gardener, hear my cries.
If you took Him from this place,
Tell me where the body lies
That I may look into His face.

JESUS [*calls, "Maria," and she turns and recognizes Him.*]

Ah, Master, grant me for a space,
As Thou are Lord and King of bliss—
Through Thy pity and Thy grace—
To give Thy holy feet a kiss.

JESUS:

Touch Me not, Mary, touch Me not,
For I must presently ascend.
But bear our friends My loving thought,
And say their cries shall have an end.
Tell My brethren I intend
To take again My heavenly power.
Say that our Father is our friend,
And I shall rise into His tower.

I go unto My Father's throne
To fit a heavenly home for you
Where mirth and happiness alone
May dwell, and joy forever new.
Man gave Me death in all men's view,
I died the death of deepest shame,
But now I bless mankind anew,
And grant him heaven through my name.

[*He goes out.*]

MAGDALENE:

No tongue can well express my bliss
Now I have seen my Lord once more.
I shall go tell my friends of this
Who swoon in sorrow, sad and sore.
I shall not hesitate therefore
But make this miracle all plain.
Now He lives forevermore
Who was lately gashed and slain.

[MAGDALENE *goes to the room on the left
where the disciples are assembled*]

Brothers, all be blithe with me.
My news for you is fair and good,
I saw Lord Jesus certainly,
A living Man in flesh and blood.
Therefore change your doubtful mood
Because our joy is now unpriced.
Though He was slain upon the rood,
I spoke right now with Jesus Christ.

PETER:

Indeed a wondrous tale this is,
But ever honored may God be!
We pray, then, Lord and King of bliss,
That we may also witness Thee
Ere Thou ascend in majesty.
Gracious God, if so it please,
Let us see Thee certainly
And set our troubled hearts at ease!

[*The scene closes.*]

Scene IV

THE LAST JUDGMENT

[CHRIST *appears surrounded by angels.* MICHAEL *bears the scales. Other angels bear the cross, nails, spear and signs of the Passion.* GABRIEL *bears his trumpet. A great crowd lies entombed on the stage and about to rise. In heaven above is seen* THE FATHER *in glory. This scene is performed with an abundance of music, pantomime and spectacle, thus taking up more time in the presentation than the brevity of the text indicates at first to the reader.*]

MICHAEL:

> *Surgite:* all men arise,
> *Venite ad judicium.*
> The judge is sitting in the skies
> And now assigns the Day of Doom.
> Prepare to meet this last assize;
> Great and small alike must come.
> Purge your souls, and well advise
> That no man there will dare be dumb.
>> Each must answer well. .
> For when God comes to question you
> The truth is bound to come to view;
> He will search it through and through
>> And send you to heaven or hell.

> Pope, prince and priest with shaven crown,
> King and kaiser, champion keen,
> Search your conscience up and down,
> For God's revenge admits no screen.
> Nor poor, nor rich of great renown,
> Not all the devils in hell's demesne,

Lout nor lady, knight nor clown,
Can keep their trespasses unseen;
  But all must come to light.
He who is found in deadly sin
Will curse the hour he entered in
And soon be devoured in devil's din,
  His doom be dealt aright.

 [THE SOULS *arise from their tombs, with vari-*
  ous cries. A crowd of DEVILS *also rushes*
  upward.]

THE SOULS:
Ha, cleave asunder, clods of clay,
Break apart and let us pass.
Now we all sing wellaway
To see our sins in heaven's glass.

THE DEVILS:
Ow, ow, ow, what shall we say?
Horror, horror, alas, alas!
Woe and alas, is this the day?
Eternal pain has come to pass.
  Terror! terror! hide our face!

THE SOULS:
Help us, Lord, or we are dead,
And let Thy mercy spring and spread.
But yet, alas, we live in dread.
  It is too late to pray for grace.

GOD:
Venite benedicti, My brethren all.
Patris mei, ye children dear!
Come hither to Me to my high hall,
All ye who held Me in righteous fear.
All foul worms from you shall fall;
With my right hand I bless you here,

Burnishing you bright as the sun's ball,
Like a keen crystal cleansing you clear,
    Your filth fades suddenly.
Peter, my servant, go you straight
To loose the locks of heaven's gate,
Let not my blessed children wait,
    But bring them glad to Me.

PETER:

The gates of heaven I open this tide.
You are welcome, dear brethren, to heaven's peace.
Come and sit on God's right side
Where mirth and melody never cease.

THE SAVED:

We creep, we crawl, we kneel, we glide,
To worship the God of all that is.
Because His wounds once gaped so wide
We now are brought to heaven's bliss.
    Holy Lord, we worship Thee!

GOD:

Welcome to Me in heaven's day,
Welcome, and never pass away,
Your happiness must ever stay.
    To mirth and joy, welcome be ye!

THE DAMNED:

Ha! ha! Mercy, mercy! we cry and crave.
Ah, mercy, Lord for our misdeed.
Ah, mercy, mercy, we roar, we rave.
Ah, help us, good Lord, in our great need!

GOD:

How can you wretches mercy have
Who cry for mercy now at need?
What have you done that I should save
Your souls? what was your merciful deed
    That mercy here might win?

FIRST DEVIL:

> Mercy, no, no, but wrath and wrack
> Shall fall upon each beaten back;
> For burnt in their brows in letters black
>   I see their secret sin.

GOD:

> To the hungry and thirsty who asked in My name
> For meat and drink, you would give none.
> You left poor naked folk in shame,
> You sought no prisoners nor men undone.
> You had no pity on sick or lame;
> You did no charity, no, not one.
> You treated the homeless man the same,
> You buried no poor man under the sun.
>   These deeds condemn you still!
> For your love I was rent on the rood,
> And for your sake I shed my blood.
> When I was so merciful and so good,
>   Why have you worked against My will?
>   [*The accusing devils now search the faces of
>   the actors and the audience.*]

SECOND DEVIL:

> Ha, ha! on your brow is clearly read
> That you were stern and stout in pride;
> That you would not give a poor man bread
> But chid him and drove him far and wide.

THIRD DEVIL:

> And in your face I see it said
> That if a thirsty man you spied
> You would rather see him dry and dead
> Before you saw his thirst supplied,
>   So covetous was your thought.

FIRST DEVIL:

> You were eager to backbite.—
> Anger was your one delight.—

You were full of poisoned spite,
　　And of sick men you reckoned nought.
SECOND DEVIL:
　Ever on envy you set your mind.
　You would never give a prisoner cheer.
　To all your neighbors you proved unkind.
　You would fail to give help, though death were near.
THIRD DEVIL:
　The sin of sloth had made you blind.
　Mass and matins you failed to hear.
　You left the dead to rot in the wind,
　And therefore you shall have endless fear,
　　　For Sloth was your favorite guest.
　You rejoiced yourself with Gluttony,
　With Riot and with Ribaldry,
　With Drinking and with Villainy,
　　　And broke good people's rest.
SECOND DEVIL:
　Sally the Slut was solace for you.
　All your life was lecherous play.
　All your neighbors knew you a shrew,
　And your pleasure was lechery every day.
　The men of God were unloved too.
　For the naked or men in poor array
　You would not spare a drop of dew,
　Or a single thread, the truth to say,
　　　When they asked in heaven's name.
THE DAMNED:
　Ah, mercy, Lord, and spare Thy might!
　We ask Thy mercy and not Thy right!
　Cover our wickedness from Thy sight!
　　　We have sinned, and we are to blame.
GOD:
　[You are unwelcome to My bliss,
　And with the devils I bid you go.

I damn you for your trespasses;
You shall live in endless woe.

THE DAMNED:

Alas, alas, that we should miss
The blessed joys God's servants know!
Alas, that we have done amiss,
And haste to wretchedness below
    Where thousand devils harm us!
            [*Amid great lamentations and cries*
        THE DEVILS *lead off* THE DAMNED
                                to hell.]

THE SAVED:

But we have risen above the skies,
Where all our bliss and gladness lies.
We greet the Lord with glad surprise:
        Te deum laudamus!] *
        [*The play ends with the singing of the* TE
        DEUM.]

---

* Since the last page of the manuscript is missing, a final stanza has been written on the analogy of the endings of similar English Mystery Plays.

Here begynneth a treatyse how þ hye
fader of heuen sendeth dethe to so=
mon euery creature to come and
gyue a counte of theyr lyues in
this worlde/and is in maner
of a morall playe.

EVERYMAN AND DEATH

From an Edition by John Skot
(c. 1530)

The Summoning of Everyman

DRAMATIS PERSONAE

GOD
EVERYMAN
DEATH
GOOD FELLOWSHIP
KINDRED
COUSIN
GOODS
GOOD DEEDS
KNOWLEDGE
CONFESSION
BEAUTY
STRENGTH
DISCRETION
FIVE WITS
MESSENGER
ANGEL
DOCTOR

[*The stage is largely bare. At the back and somewhat to
one side is a tomb. In a balcony at the rear centre of the
stage is a representation of heaven, wherein* GOD *and* HIS
ANGELS *are seated. A* MESSENGER *enters as a prologue.*]

MESSENGER:
    I pray you all, give your audience,
    And hear this matter with reverence,
    By figure of a moral play.
    The Summoning of Everyman called it is,
    That of our lives and ending shows

How transitory we be all day.
This matter is wondrous precious
But the meaning of it is more gracious
And sweet to bear away.
The story saith: Man, in the beginning
Look well and take good heed to the ending,
Be you never so gay!
Ye think sin in the beginning full sweet,
Which in the end causeth the soul to weep
When the body lieth in clay.
Here shall you see how Fellowship and Jollity,
Both Strength, Pleasure and Beauty,
Will fade from thee as flower in May;
For ye shall hear how our heavenly King
Calleth Everyman to a general reckoning.
Give audience and hear what He doth say.

GOD:

I perceive, here in My majesty,
How that all creatures be to Me unkind,
Living without dread in worldly prosperity.
Of ghostly sight the people be so blind,
Drowned in sin, they know Me not for God.
In worldly riches is all their mind;
They fear not My righteousness, the sharp rod;
My love that I showed when I for them died
They forget clean, and shedding of my blood red;
I hanged between two, it cannot be denied;
To get them life I suffered to be dead;
I healed their feet: with thorns hurt was My head.
I could no more than I did, truly.
And now I see the people do clean forsake Me.
They use the seven deadly sins damnable,
As pride, covetise, wrath and lechery,
Now in the world be made commendable;

And thus they leave of angels, the heavenly com-
pany.
Every man liveth so after his own pleasure,
And yet of their life they be nothing sure.
I see the more that I them forbear,
The worse they be from year to year.
All that liveth declineth fast,
Therefore I will in all haste
Have a reckoning of every man's person;
For, if I leave the people thus alone
In their life and wicked tempests,
Verily they will become much worse than beasts;
For now one would by envy another eat up;
Charity they do all clean forget.
I hoped well that every man
In My glory should make his mansion,
And thereto I had them all elect;
But now I see, like traitors deject,
They thank Me not for the pleasure that I to them
meant,
Nor yet for their being that I them have lent;
I proffered the people great multitude of mercy.
And few there be that ask it heartily;
They be so cumbered with wordly riches,
That needs on them I must do justice,
On every man living without fear.
Where art thou, Death, thou mighty messenger?

[DEATH *enters.*]

DEATH:

Almighty God, I am here at Your will,
Your commandment to fulfill.

GOD:

Go thou to Everyman,
And show him in My name

A pilgrimage he must on him take,
Which he in no wise may escape;
And that he bring with him a sure reckoning
Without delay or any tarrying.

DEATH:

Lord, I will in the world go run over all,
And cruelly out-search both great and small;
Every man will I beset that liveth beastly,
Against God's laws, and dreadeth not folly:
He that loveth riches I will strike with my dart,
His sight to blind, and from heaven to depart,
Except that alms be his good friend,
In hell for to dwell, world without end.

[*Enter* EVERYMAN.]

Lo, yonder I see Everyman walking:
Full little he thinketh on my coming:
His mind is on fleshly lusts and his treasure;
And great pain it shall cause him to endure
Before the Lord, heaven's King.
Everyman, stand still; whither art thou going
Thus gaily? hast thou thy Maker forgot?

EVERYMAN:

Why askest thou? Wouldest thou wit?

DEATH:

Yea, sir, I will show you; in great haste I am sent
to thee
From God out of His majesty.

EVERYMAN:

What! sent to me?

DEATH:

Yea, certainly:
Though thou hast forgot Him here,
He thinketh on thee in the heavenly sphere;
As, ere we depart, thou shalt know.

EVERYMAN:

What desireth God of me?

DEATH:

That shall I show thee;
A reckoning He will needs have
Without any longer respite.

EVERYMAN:

To give a reckoning longer leisure I crave;
This blind matter troubleth my wit.

DEATH:

On thee thou must take a long journey,
Therefore thy book of count with thee thou bring,
For turn again thou cannot by no way:
And look thou be sure of thy reckoning;
For before God thou shalt answer and show
Thy many bad deeds, and good but a few,
How thou hast spent thy life, and in what wise,
Before the Chief Lord of Paradise.
Have ado that we were in that way,
For, wit thou well, thou shalt make none attorney.

EVERYMAN:

Full unready I am such reckoning to give:
I know thee not; what messenger art thou?

DEATH:

I am Death, who no man dreadeth;
For every man I arrest, and no man spare,
For it is God's commandment
That all to me should be obedient.

EVERYMAN:

O Death, thou comest, when I had thee least in mind;
In thy power it lieth me to save;
Yet of my good will I give thee, if you wilt be kind,
Yea, a thousand pounds shalt thou have,
If thou defer this matter till another day.

DEATH:

> Everyman, it may not be by no way;
> I set naught by gold, silver, nor riches,
> Nor by pope, emperor, king, duke, nor princes;
> For, if I would receive gifts great,
> All the world I might get;
> But my custom is clean contrary;
> I give thee no respite; come hence, and not tarry.

EVERYMAN:

> Alas! shall I have no longer respite?
> I may say Death giveth no warning:
> To think on thee it maketh my heart sick;
> For all unready is my book of reckoning:
> But, for twelve years, if I might have abiding,
> My counting book I would make so clear,
> That my reckoning I should not need to fear.
> Wherefore, Death, I pray thee for God's mercy,
> Spare me, till I be provided of remedy.

DEATH:

> Thee availeth not to cry, weep, and pray:
> But haste thee lightly, that thou wert gone that
>   journey;
> And prove thy friends, if thou can;
> For, wit thou well, the tide abideth no man,
> And in the world each living creature
> For Adam's sin must die of nature.

EVERYMAN:

> Death, if I should this pilgrimage take,
> And my reckoning surely make,
> Show me, for Saint Charity,
> Should I not come again shortly?

DEATH:

> No, Everyman, if thou be once there,
> Thou mayest never more come here,
> Trust me verily.

EVERYMAN:

> O gracious God, in the high seat celestial,
> Have mercy on me in this most need!
> Shall I have no company from this vale terrestrial
> Of mine acquaintance, that way me to lead?

DEATH:

> Yea, if any be so hardy,
> That would go with thee, and bear thee company:
> Hie thee that thou wert gone to God's magnificence,
> Thy reckoning to give before His presence.
> What, thoughtest thou thy life is given thee,
> And thy worldly goods also?

EVERYMAN:

> I had thought so verily.

DEATH:

> Nay, nay; it was but lent thee;
> For, as soon as thou art gone,
> Another awhile shall have it, and then go therefrom,
> Even as thou hast done.
> Everyman, thou art mad, thou hast thy wits five,
> And here on earth wilt not amend thy life;
> For suddenly I do come.

EVERYMAN:

> O wretched caitiff, whither shall I flee,
> That I might escape this endless sorrow!
> Now, gentle Death, spare me till to-morrow,
> That I may amend me
> With good advisement.

DEATH:

> Nay, thereto I will not consent,
> Nor no man will I respite;
> But to the heart suddenly I shall smite
> Without any advisement.
> And now out of thy sight I will me hie;
> See thou make thee ready shortly,

For thou mayest say, this is the day
That no man living may escape away.

[DEATH *goes out.*]

EVERYMAN:

Alas! I may well weep with sighs deep:
Now have I no manner of company
To help me in my journey, and me to keep;
And also my writing is full unready.
How shall I do now for to excuse me!
I would to God I had never been begot;
To my soul a full great profit it had been,
For now I fear pains huge and great.
The time passeth: Lord, help, Who all wrought!
For though I mourn, it availeth nought:
The day passeth, and is almost ago;
I wot not well what for to do.
To whom were I best my complaint to make?
What, if I to Fellowship thereof spake,
And showed him of this sudden chance!
For in him is all mine affiance.

[*Enter* FELLOWSHIP.]

We have in the world so many a day
Been good friends in sport and play.
I see him yonder certainly;
I trust that he will bear me company;
Therefore to him will I speak to ease my sorrow,
Well met, good Fellowship, and good morrow.

FELLOWSHIP:

Everyman, good morrow, by this day:
Sir, why lookest thou so piteously?
If anything be amiss, I pray thee, me say,
That I may help to remedy.

EVERYMAN:

Yea, good Fellowship, yea;
I am in great jeopardy.

FELLOWSHIP:
> My true friend, show to me your mind;
> I will not forsake thee, to my life's end,
> In the way of good company.

EVERYMAN:
> That was well spoken and lovingly.

FELLOWSHIP:
> Sir, I must needs know your heaviness;
> I have pity to see you in any distress:
> If any have you wronged, ye shall revenged be,
> Though I on the ground be slain for thee;
> Though that I know before that I should die.

EVERYMAN:
> Verily, Fellowship, gramercy.

FELLOWSHIP:
> Tush, by thy thanks I set not a straw;
> Show me thy grief, and say no more.

EVERYMAN:
> If I my heart should to you break,
> And then you should turn your mind from me,
> And would not me comfort, when ye hear me speak,
> Then should I ten times sorrier be.

FELLOWSHIP:
> Sir, I say as I will do in deed.

EVERYMAN:
> Then be you a good friend at need;
> I have found you true here-before.

FELLOWSHIP:
> And so ye shall evermore;
> For in faith, if thou go to hell,
> I will not forsake thee by the way.

EVERYMAN:
> Ye speak like a good friend, I believe you well;
> I shall deserve it, if I may.

FELLOWSHIP:

I speak of no deserving, by this day;
For he that will say and nothing do,
Is not worthy with good company to go:
Therefore show me the grief of your mind,
As to your friend most loving and kind.

EVERYMAN:

I shall show you how it is:
Commanded I am to go a journey,
A long way, hard and dangerous;
And give a strait account without delay
Before the High Judge Adonai;
Wherefore, I pray you, bear me company,
As ye have promised in this journey.

FELLOWSHIP:

That is matter indeed; promise is duty;
But, if I should take such a voyage on me,
I know it well, it should be to my pain:
Also it makes me afraid certain.
But let us take counsel here as well as we can,
For your words would fear a strong man.

EVERYMAN:

Why, ye said if I had need,
Ye would me never forsake quick nor dead,
Though it were to hell truly.

FELLOWSHIP:

So I said certainly;
But such pleasures be set aside, the sooth to say,
And also if ye took such a journey,
When should we come again?

EVERYMAN:

Nay, never again till the day of doom.

FELLOWSHIP:

In faith, then will not I come there:
Who hath you these tidings brought?

EVERYMAN:
 Indeed, Death was with me here.
FELLOWSHIP:
 Now, by God that all hath bought,
 If Death were the messenger,
 For no man that is living to-day
 I will not go that loath journey,
 Not for the father that begat me.
EVERYMAN:
 Ye promised otherwise, pardy.
FELLOWSHIP:
 I wot well I said so truly,
 And yet if thou wilt eat and drink, and make good
  cheer,
 Or haunt to women the lusty company,
 I would not forsake you, while the day is clear,
 Trust me verily.
EVERYMAN:
 Yea, thereto ye would be ready;
 To go to mirth, solace and play,
 Your mind will sooner apply
 Than to bear me company in my long journey.
FELLOWSHIP:
 Now, in good faith, I will not that way;
 But, if thou will murder, or any man kill,
 In that I will help thee with a good will.
EVERYMAN:
 Oh, that is a simple advice indeed:
 Gentle Fellowship, help me in my necessity;
 We have loved long, and now I need,
 And now, gentle Fellowship, remember me.
FELLOWSHIP:
 Whether ye have loved me or no,
 By Saint John, I will not with thee go.

EVERYMAN:

> Yet, I pray thee, take the labor, and do so much for
>   me,
> To bring me forward, for Saint Charity,
> And comfort me, till I come without the town.

FELLOWSHIP:

> Nay, if thou wouldst give me a new gown,
> I will not a foot with thee go;
> But, if thou hadst tarried, I would not have left thee
>   so:
> And as now God speed thee in thy journey!
> For from thee I will depart, as fast as I may.

EVERYMAN:

> Whither away, Fellowship? wilt thou forsake me?

FELLOWSHIP:

> Yea, by my fay; to God I commend thee.

EVERYMAN:

> Farewell, good Fellowship; for thee my heart is
>   sore:
> Adieu for ever, I shall see thee no more.

FELLOWSHIP:

> In faith, Everyman, farewell now at the end;
> For you I will remember parting is mourning.
>
> > [FELLOWSHIP *goes out.*]

EVERYMAN:

> Alack! shall we thus depart indeed,
> O Lady, help! without any more comfort,
> Lo, Fellowship forsaketh me in my most need:
> For help in this world whither shall I resort?
> Fellowship here before with me would merry make;
> And now little sorrow for me doth he take.
> It is said, in prosperity men friends may find,
> Which in adversity be full unkind.
> Now whither for succour shall I flee,
> Since Fellowship hath forsaken me?

To my kinsmen I will truly,
Praying them to help me in my necessity;
I believe that they will do so;
For kind will creep, where it may not go.
I will go try; for yonder I see them go:
Where be ye now, my friends and kinsmen lo?

                              [KINDRED *and* COUSIN *enter.*]

KINDRED:

Here be we now at your commandment:
Cousin, I pray thee, show us your intent
In any wise, and do not spare.

COUSIN:

Yea, Everyman, and to us declare
If ye be disposed to go any whither;
For, wot ye well, we will live and die together.

KINDRED:

In wealth and woe we will with you hold,
For over his kin a man may be bold.

EVERYMAN:

Gramercy, my friends and kinsmen kind,
Now shall I show you the grief of my mind.
I was commanded by a messenger,
That is an high king's chief officer;
He bade me go on pilgrimage to my pain,
But I know well I shall never come again:
Also I must give a reckoning strait;
For I have a great enemy that hath me in wait,
Which intendeth me for to hinder.

KINDRED:

What account is that which ye must render?
That would I know.

EVERYMAN:

Of all my works I must show,
How I have lived, and my days spent;
Also of ill deeds that I have used

In my time since life was me lent,
And of all virtues that I have refused:
Therefore, I pray you, go thither with me
To help to make mine account, for Saint Charity.

COUSIN:

What, to go thither? Is that the matter?
Nay, Everyman, I had liever fast bread and water,
All this five year and more.

EVERYMAN:

Alas, that ever I was bore!
For now shall I never be merry,
If that you forsake me.

KINDRED:

Ah, sir! what, ye be a merry man!
Take good heart to you, and make no moan.
But one thing I warn you, by Saint Anne,
As for me, ye shall go alone.

EVERYMAN:

My cousin, will you not with me go?

COUSIN:

No, by our lady, I have a cramp in my toe:
Trust not to me; for, so God me speed,
I will deceive you in your most need.

KINDRED:

It availeth not us to entice;
Ye shall have my maid with all my heart;
She loveth to go to feasts, there to be nice,
And to dance, and abroad to start:
I will give her leave to help you in that journey,
If that you and she may agree.

EVERYMAN:

No, show me the very effect of your mind;
Will you go with me, or abide behind?

KINDRED:

    Abide behind! yea, that will I, if I may;
    Therefore farewell till another day.

                                   [KINDRED *goes out.*]

EVERYMAN:

    How should I be merry or glad?
    For fair promises men to me make;
    But, when I have most need, they me forsake;
    I am deceived, that maketh me sad.

COUSIN:

    Cousin Everyman, farewell now;
    For verily I will not go with you:
    Also of mine own life an unready reckoning
    I have to account, therefore I make tarrying;
    Now God keep thee, for now I go.

                                   [COUSIN *goes out.*]

EVERYMAN:

    Ah, Jesu, is all come hereto?
    Lo, fair words make fools fain;
    They promise, and nothing will do certain.
    My kinsmen promised me faithfully,
    For to abide with me steadfastly;
    And now fast away do they flee:
    Even so Fellowship promised me.
    What friend were best me now to provide?
    I lose my time here longer to abide;
    Yet in my mind a thing there is:
    All my life I have loved riches;
    If that my Goods now help me might,
    It would make my heart full light:
    I will speak to him in this distress:
    Where art thou, my Goods and Riches?

                                   [GOODS *enters.*]

GOODS:

> Who calleth me? Everyman? what, hast thou haste?
> I lie here in corners trussed and piled so high,
> And in chests I am locked fast,
> Also sacked in bags, thou mayest see with thine eye,
> I cannot stir; in packs, lo, where I lie!
> What would ye have, lightly me say.

EVERYMAN:

> Come hither, Goods, in all the haste thou may;
> For of counsel I must desire thee.

GOODS:

> Sir, if ye in the world have sorrow or adversity,
> That can I help you to remedy shortly.

EVERYMAN:

> It is another disease that grieveth me;
> In this world it is not, I tell thee so,
> I am sent for another way to go,
> To give a strait account general
> Before the highest Jupiter of all:
> And all my life I have had joy and pleasure in thee,
> Therefore I pray thee, go with me;
> For, peradventure, thou mayest before God
>   Almighty
> My reckoning help to clean and purify,
> For it is said ever among,
> That money maketh all right that is wrong.

GOODS:

> Nay, Everyman, I sing another song;
> I follow no man in such voyages,
> For, if I went with thee,
> Thou shouldest fare much the worse for me:
> For because on me thou didst set thy mind,
> Thy reckoning I have made blotted and blind,

That thine account thou cannot make truly;
And that hast thou for the love of me.

EVERYMAN:

That would grieve me full sore,
When I should come to that fearful answer:
Up, and let us go thither together.

GOODS:

Nay, not so; I am too brittle, I may not endure:
I will follow no man on foot, be ye sure.

EVERYMAN:

Alas! I have thee loved, and had great pleasure
All my life-days on my goods and treasure.

GOODS:

That is to thy damnation, without lying,
For my love is contrary to the love everlasting;
But if thou had me loved moderately during,
As to the poor given part of me,
Then shouldest thou not in this dolour have been,
Nor in this great sorrow and care.

EVERYMAN:

Lo, now was I deceived, ere I was aware,
And all, I may see, mis-spending of time.

GOODS:

What, thinkest thou that I am thine?

EVERYMAN:

I had thought so.

GOODS:

Nay, Everyman, I say no:
As for a while I was lent thee;
A season thou hast had me in prosperity;
My condition is man's soul to kill;
If I save one, a thousand I do spill:
Deemest thou that I will follow thee?
Nay, not from this world, verily.

EVERYMAN:

I had thought otherwise.

GOODS:

Therefore to thy soul Goods is a thief,
For when thou art dead, this is my guise,
Another to deceive in the same wise,
As I have done thee, and all to his soul's grief.

EVERYMAN:

O false Goods, cursed mayst thou be,
Thou traitor to God, thou hast deceived me,
And caught me in thy snare.

GOODS:

Marry, thou broughtst thyself in care,
Whereof I am right glad:
I must needs laugh, I cannot be sad.

EVERYMAN:

Ah, Goods, thou hast had long my hearty love;
I gave thee that which should be the Lord's above:
But wilt thou not go with me indeed?
I pray thee truth to say.

GOODS:

No, so God me speed;
Therefore farewell, and have good day.

[GOODS *goes out.*]

EVERYMAN:

Oh, to whom shall I make my moan,
For to go with me in that heavy journey?
First Fellowship said he would with me go;
His words were very pleasant and gay,
But afterwards he left me alone.
Then spake I to my kinsmen all in despair,
And also they gave me words fair,
They lacked no fair speaking;
But all forsake me in the ending.

Then went I to my Goods that I loved best,
In hope to have found comfort; but there had I
    least:
For my Goods sharply did me tell,
That he bringeth many in hell.
Then of myself I was ashamed,
And so I am worthy to be blamed:
Thus may I well myself hate.
Of whom shall I now counsel take?
I think that I shall never speed,
Till that I go to my Good Deed;
But, alas! she is so weak,
That she can neither go nor speak:
Yet will I venture on her now.
My Good Deeds, where be you?

                              [GOOD DEEDS *enters*.]

GOOD DEEDS:
Here I lie cold in the ground;
Thy sins have me so sore bound,
That I cannot stir.

EVERYMAN:
O Good Deeds, I stand in fear;
I must you pray of counsel,
For help now should come right well.

GOOD DEEDS:
Everyman, I have understanding,
That thou art summoned account to make
Before Messias of Jerusalem King;
If you do by me, that journey with you will I take.

EVERYMAN:
Therefore I come to you my moan to make:
I pray you, that ye will go with me.

GOOD DEEDS:
I would full fain, but I cannot stand, verily.

EVERYMAN:

Why, is there anything on you fallen?

GOOD DEEDS:

Yea, sir, I may thank you for all;
If ye had perfectly cheered me,
Your book of account full ready now had been.
Look, the books of your works and deeds eke!
Behold how they lie under the feet,
To your soul's heaviness.

EVERYMAN:

Our Lord Jesus help me!
For one letter herein can I not see.

GOOD DEEDS:

Here is a blind reckoning in time of distress!

EVERYMAN:

Good Deeds, I pray you, help me in this need,
Or else I am for ever damned indeed;
Therefore help me to make my reckoning
Before the Redeemer of all thing,
Who is, and was, and ever shall be King.

GOOD DEEDS:

Everyman, I am sorry for your fall,
And fain would I help you, if I were able.

EVERYMAN:

Good Deeds, your counsel, I pray you, give me.

GOOD DEEDS:

That shall I do verily:
Though on my feet I may not go,
I have a sister that shall with you also,
Called Knowledge, which shall with you abide,
To help you to make that dreadful reckoning.

[*Enter* KNOWLEDGE.]

KNOWLEDGE:

Everyman, I will go with thee, and be thy guide,
In thy most need to go by thy side.

EVERYMAN:

    In good condition I am now in every thing,

    And am wholly content with this good thing,

    Thanked be God my Creator.

GOOD DEEDS:

    And when he hath brought thee there,

    Where thou shalt heal thee of thy smart,

    Then go thou with thy reckoning and thy good deeds

      together,

    For to make thee joyful at heart

    Before the blessed Trinity.

EVERYMAN:

    My Good Deeds, I thank thee heartfully:

    I am well content certainly

    With your words sweet.

KNOWLEDGE:

    Now go we together lovingly

    To Confession, that cleansing river.

EVERYMAN:

    For joy I weep: I would that we were there;

    But I pray you to instruct me by intellection,

    Where dwelleth that holy virtue Confession?

KNOWLEDGE:

    In the house of salvation;

    We shall find him in that place,

    That shall us comfort by God's grace.

                 [CONFESSION *enters.*]

    Lo, this is Confession: kneel down, and ask mercy;

    For he is in good conceit with God Almighty.

EVERYMAN:

    O glorious fountain that all uncleanness doth clarify,

    Wash from me the spots of vices unclean,

    That on me no sin may be seen;

    I come with Knowledge for my redemption,

    With heart's repentance and full contrition,

For I am commanded a pilgrimage to take.
And great accounts before God to make.
Now, I pray you, Shrift, mother of salvation,
Help my good deeds at my piteous exclamation.

CONFESSION:

I know your sorrow well, Everyman:
Because with Knowledge ye come to me,
I will comfort you as well as I can;
And a precious jewel I will give thee,
Called penance, voider of adversity:
Therewith shall your body chastised be,
With abstinence and perseverance in God's service;
Here shall you receive that scourge of me,
Which is strong penance that ye must endure;
Remember thy Savior was scourged for thee
With sharp scourges, and suffered it patiently:
So must thou, ere thou pass that painful pilgrimage.
Knowledge, keep him in this voyage,
And by the time Good Deeds will be with thee;
But in anywise be sure of mercy,
For your time draweth fast, if ye will saved be,
Ask God mercy, and He will grant truly:
When with the scourge of penance man doth him
        bind,
The oil of forgiveness then shall he find.

EVERYMAN:

Thanked be God for His gracious work;
For now I will my penance begin:
This hath rejoiced and lighted my heart,
Though the knots be painful and hard within.

KNOWLEDGE:

Everyman, look your penance that ye fulfill,
What pain that ever it to you be;
And Knowledge shall give you counsel at will,
How your account ye shall make clearly.

EVERYMAN:

O eternal God, O heavenly figure,
O way of righteousness, O goodly vision,
Which descended down in a virgin pure,
Because He would Everyman redeem,
Which Adam forfeited by his disobedience,
O blessed Godhead, elect and high Divine,
Forgive me my grievous offence;
Here I cry thee mercy in this presence:
O ghostly Treasure, O Ransomer and Redeemer!
Of all the world Hope and Conducter,
Mirror of joy, Foundation of mercy,
Which enlumineth heaven and earth thereby,
Hear my clamorous complaint, though it late be,
Receive my prayers unworthy of Thy benignity,
Though I be a sinner most abominable,
Yet let my name be written in Moses' table.
O Mary, pray to the Maker of all things
Me for to help at my ending,
And save me from the power of my enemy;
For Death assaileth me strongly:
And, Lady, that I may by means of thy prayer
Of your Son's glory be partner.
By the means of His passion I it crave;
I beseech you help me my soul to save.
Knowledge, give me the scourge of penance,
My flesh therewith shall give acquittance;
I will now begin, if God give me grace.

KNOWLEDGE:

Everyman, God give you time and space!
Thus I bequeath you in the hands of our Savior;
Now may you make your reckoning sure.

EVERYMAN:

In the name of all the Holy Trinity,
My body punished sore shall be.

Take this, body, for the sin of the flesh;
Also thou delightest to go gay and fresh;
And in the way of damnation thou didst me bring,
Therefore suffer now strokes and punishing:
Now of penance I will wade the water clear,
To save me from purgatory, that sharp fire.

GOOD DEEDS:

I thank God, now I can walk and go,
And am delivered of my sickness and woe;
Therefore with Everyman I will go, and not spare;
His good works I will help him to declare.

KNOWLEDGE:

Now, Everyman, be merry and glad;
Your Good Deeds cometh now, ye may not be sad:
Now is your Good Deeds whole and sound,
Going upright upon the ground.

EVERYMAN:

My heart is light, and shall be evermore;
Now will I smite faster than I did before.

GOOD DEEDS:

Everyman pilgrim, my special friend,
Blessed be thou without end;
For thee is prepared the eternal glory:
Ye have made me whole and sound,
Therefore I will bide by thee in every ground.

EVERYMAN:

Welcome, my Good Deeds, now I hear thy voice,
I weep for very sweetness of love.

KNOWLEDGE:

Be no more sad, but evermore rejoice,
God seeth thy living in His throne above,
Put on this garment to thy behove,
Which with your tears is now all wet,
Lest before God it be unsweet,
When ye to your journey's end shall come.

EVERYMAN:

Gentle Knowledge, what do ye it call?

KNOWLEDGE:

It is the garment of sorrow,
From pain it will you borrow;
Contrition it is,
That getteth forgiveness,
It pleaseth God passing well.

GOOD DEEDS:

Everyman, will you wear it for your health?

EVERYMAN:

Now blessed be Jesu, Mary's son;
For now have I on true contrition:
And let us go now without tarrying.
Good Deeds, have we cleared our reckoning?

GOOD DEEDS:

Yea, indeed, I have here.

EVERYMAN:

Then I trust we need not to fear;
Now, friends, let us not part in twain.

KNOWLEDGE:

Nay, Everyman, that will we not certain.

GOOD DEEDS:

Yet must thou lead with thee
Three persons of great might.

EVERYMAN:

Who should they be?

GOOD DEEDS:

Discretion and Strength they hyght,
And thy Beauty may not abide behind.

KNOWLEDGE:

Also ye must call to mind
Your Five Wits as your councillors.

GOOD DEEDS:

You must have them ready at all hours.

EVERYMAN:

> How shall I get them hither?

KNOWLEDGE:

> You must call them all together
> And they will hear you incontinent.

EVERYMAN:

> My friends, come hither, and be present,
> Discretion, Strength, My Five Wits, and Beauty.
> > [*Enter* DISCRETION, STRENGTH, FIVE
> > WITS, *and* BEAUTY.]

BEAUTY:

> Here at your will we be all ready;
> What will ye that we should do?

GOOD DEEDS:

> That ye would with Everyman go,
> And help him in his pilgrimage:
> Advise you, will ye go with him or not in that
> voyage?

STRENGTH:

> We will bring him all thither
> To help and comfort him, ye may believe me.

DISCRETION:

> So will we go with him all together.

EVERYMAN:

> Almighty God, loved may Thou be;
> I give Thee praise that I have hither brought
> Strength, Discretion, Beauty, Five Wits: lack I
> nought:
> And my Good Deeds, with Knowledge clear,
> All be in my company at my will here;
> I desire no more to my business.

STRENGTH:

> And I, Strength, will by you stand in distress,
> Though thou wouldest in battle fight on the ground.

FIVE WITS:

> And though it were through the world round
> We will not depart for sweet nor sour.

BEAUTY:

> No more will I unto death's hour,
> Whatsoever thereof befall.

DISCRETION:

> Everyman, advise you first of all,
> Go with a good advisement and deliberation;
> We all give you virtuous admonition
> That all shall be well.

EVERYMAN:

> My friends, hark what I will you tell;
> I pray God reward you in His heavenly sphere:
> Now hearken all that be here;
> For I will make my testament
> Here before you all present:
> In alms half my goods I will give with my hands
>   twain
> In the way of charity with good intent,
> And the other half still shall remain:
> I it bequeath to be returned where it ought to be.
> This I do in despite of the fiend of hell,
> To go quit out of his peril
> Ever after this day.

KNOWLEDGE:

> Everyman, hearken what I will say;
> Go to priesthood, I you advise,
> And receive of him in any wise
> The holy Sacrament and ointment together,
> Then shortly see ye turn again hither;
> We will all abide you here.

FIVE WITS:

> Yea, Everyman, hie you that ye ready were:
> There is no emperor, king, duke nor baron,

That of God hath commission,
As hath the least priest in the world being;
For of the Sacraments pure and benign
He beareth the keys, and thereof hath cure
For man's redemption, it is ever sure,
Which God for our soul's medicine
Gave us out of His heart with great pain,
Here in this transitory life for thee and me:
The blessed Sacraments seven there be,
Baptism, confirmation, with priesthood good,
And the Sacrament of God's precious flesh and
    blood,
Marriage, the holy extreme unction, and penance;
These seven be good to have in remembrance,
Gracious Sacraments of high divinity.

EVERYMAN:

Fain would I receive that holy Body,
And meekly to my ghostly father I will go.

FIVE WITS:

Everyman, that is the best that ye can do;
God will you to salvation bring,
For good priesthood exceedeth all other thing;
To us Holy Scripture they do teach,
And convert man from sin, heaven to reach;
God hath to them more power given
Than to any angel that is in heaven:
With five words he may consecrate
God's body in flesh and blood to make,
And handleth his Maker between his hands.
The priest bindeth and unbindeth all bands
Both in earth and in heaven;
He ministers all the Sacraments seven:
Though we kiss thy feet, thou wert worthy:
Thou art the surgeon that cureth sin deadly,

No remedy may we find under God,
But all only priesthood.
Everyman, God gave priests that dignity,
And setteth them in His stead among us to be;
Thus be they above angels in degree.

[EVERYMAN *goes out to receive*
the Sacrament.]

KNOWLEDGE:

If priests be good, it is so surely,
But when Jesu hung on the cross with great smart,
There He gave us out of His blessed heart
The same Sacrament in great torment.
He sold them not to us, that Lord omnipotent;
Therefore Saint Peter the Apostle doth say,
That Jesus' curse have all they,
Who God their Savior do buy or sell,
Or they for any money do take or tell.
Sinful priests give the sinners example bad;
Their children sit by other men's fires, I have heard,
And some haunt women's company,
With unclean life, as lusts of lechery;
These are with sin made blind.

FIVE WITS:

I trust to God no such may we find:
Therefore let us priesthood honor,
And follow their doctrine for our soul's succor;
We be their sheep, and they shepherds be,
By whom we all be kept in surety.
Peace! for yonder I see Everyman come,
Who hath made true satisfaction.

GOOD DEEDS:

Methinks it is he indeed.

[EVERYMAN *enters.*]

EVERYMAN:

> Now Jesu Christ be your speed!
> I have received the Sacrament for my redemption,
> And then mine extreme unction;
> Blessed be all they that counseled me to take it:
> And now, friends, let us go without longer respite;
> I thank God that ye have tarried so long.
> Now set each of you on this rod your hand,
> And shortly follow me;
> I go before, there I would be:
> God be our guide.

STRENGTH:

> Everyman, we will not from you go,
> Till ye have gone this voyage long.

DISCRETION:

> I, Discretion, will bide by you also.

KNOWLEDGE:

> And though this pilgrimage be never so strong,
> I will never part you from:
> Everyman, I will be as sure by thee,
> As ever I was by Judas Maccabee.

EVERYMAN:

> Alas! I am so faint I may not stand,
> My limbs under me do fold:
> Friends, let us not turn again to this land,
> Not for all the world's gold;
> For into this cave must I creep,
> And turn to the earth, and there to sleep.

BEAUTY:

> What, into this grave? Alas!

EVERYMAN:

> Yea, there shall ye consume more and less.

BEAUTY:

> And what, should I smother here?

EVERYMAN:

Yea, by my faith, and never more appear;
In this world live no more we shall,
But in heaven before the highest Lord of all.

BEAUTY:

I cross out all this: adieu, by Saint John;
I take my cap in my lap, and am gone.

EVERYMAN:

What, Beauty? whither will ye?

BEAUTY:

Peace! I am deaf, I look not behind me,
Not if thou wouldst give me all the gold in thy chest.
                                    [BEAUTY *goes out.*]

EVERYMAN:

Alas! whereto may I now trust?
Beauty doth fast away hie:
She promised with me to live and die.

STRENGTH:

Everyman, I will thee also forsake and deny,
The game liketh me not at all.

EVERYMAN:

Why then ye will forsake me all:
Sweet Strength, tarry a little space.

STRENGTH:

Nay, sir, by the cross of grace,
I will hie me from thee fast,
Though thou weep till thy heart brast.

EVERYMAN:

Ye would ever bide by me, ye said.

STRENGTH:

Yea, I have you far enough conveyed:
Ye be old enough, I understand,
Your pilgrimage to take on hand;
I repent me, that I hither came.

EVERYMAN:

    Strength, you to displease I am to blame;

    Yet promise is debt; this ye well wot.

STRENGTH:

    In faith, as for that I care not:

    Thou art but a fool to complain;

    Thou spendest thy speech and wastest thy brain:

    Go, thrust thee into the ground.

                  [STRENGTH *goes out.*]

EVERYMAN:

    I had thought surer I should you have found:

    He that trusteth in his Strength

    Is greatly deceived at the length;

    Both Strength and Beauty have forsaken me,

    Yet they promised me steadfast to be.

DISCRETION:

    Everyman, I will after Strength be gone;

    As for me, I will leave you alone.

EVERYMAN:

    Why, Discretion, will ye forsake me?

DISCRETION:

    Yea, in faith, I will go from thee;

    For when Strength is gone before,

    Then I follow after evermore.

EVERYMAN:

    Yet, I pray thee, for love of the Trinity,

    Look in my grave once piteously.

DISCRETION:

    Nay, so nigh will I not come.

    Now, farewell, fellows everyone.

                [DISCRETION *goes out.*]

EVERYMAN:

    Oh, all things fail, save God alone,

    Beauty, Strength and Discretion;

For, when Death bloweth his blast,
They all run from me full fast.

FIVE WITS:

Everyman, of thee now my leave I take;
I will follow the other, for here I thee forsake.

EVERYMAN:

Alas! then may I both wail and weep;
For I took you for my best friend.

FIVE WITS:

I will no longer thee keep:
Now farewell, and here an end.

[FIVE WITS *goes out*.]

EVERYMAN:

Now, Jesu, help! all have forsaken me.

GOOD DEEDS:

Nay, Everyman, I will abide with thee,
I will not forsake thee indeed;
Thou shalt find me a good friend at need.

EVERYMAN:

Gramercy, Good Deeds, now may I true friends see.
They have forsaken me, everyone;
I loved them better than my good deeds alone:
Knowledge, will ye forsake me also?

KNOWLEDGE:

Yea, Everyman, when ye to death shall go;
But not yet for no manner of danger.

EVERYMAN:

Gramercy, Knowledge, with all my heart.

KNOWLEDGE:

Nay, yet I will not from hence depart,
Till I see where ye shall be come.

EVERYMAN:

Methinketh, alas! that I must be gone
To make my reckoning, and my debts pay;

For I see my time is nigh spent away.
Take example, all ye that this do hear or see,
How they that I loved best now forsake me;
Except my Good Deeds, that bideth truly.

GOOD DEEDS:

All earthly things are but vanity,
Beauty, Strength, and Discretion do man forsake,
Foolish friends and kinsmen, that fair spake;
All flee save Good Deeds, and that am I.

EVERYMAN:

Have mercy on me, God most mighty,
And stand by me, thou mother and maid, Holy
Mary!

GOOD DEEDS:

Fear not, I will speak for thee.

EVERYMAN:

Here I cry God mercy!

GOOD DEEDS:

Cut our end and minish our pain:
Let us go, and never come again.

EVERYMAN:

Into Thy hands, Lord, my soul I commend;
Receive it, Lord, that it be not lost;
As Thou me boughtest, so me defend,
And save me from the fiend's boast,
That I may appear with that blessed host
That shall be saved at the day of doom:
In manus tuas, of might most,
For ever *commendo spiritum meum.*

[EVERYMAN *and* GOOD DEEDS *descend
into the grave.*]

KNOWLEDGE:

Now hath he suffered what we all shall endure:
The Good Deeds shall make all sure;

Now hath he made ending,
Methinketh that I hear angels sing,
And make great joy and melody,
Where Everyman's soul shall received be.
                              [KNOWLEDGE *goes out.*]

THE ANGEL:
Come, excellent elect spouse to Jesu,
Here above thou shalt go,
Because of thy singular virtue:
Now thy soul is taken thy body from,
Thy reckoning is crystal clear;
Now shalt thou into the heavenly sphere,
Unto the which all ye shall come
Who live well, after the day of doom.
                       [*A* DOCTOR OF DIVINITY *enters.*]

DOCTOR:
This memory all men may have in mind;
Ye hearers, take it of worth, old and young,
And forsake pride, for he deceiveth you in the end,
And remember Beauty, Five Wits, Strength and Dis-
    cretion,
They all at last do Everyman forsake,
Save his Good Deeds, there doth he none take:
But beware, for if they be small,
Before God he hath no help at all;
No excuse may be there for Everyman:
Alas, how shall he do then?
For after death amends may no man make,
For then mercy and pity do him forsake;
If his reckoning be not clear, when he doth come,
God will say, *Ite, maledicti, in ignem aeternum;*
And he that hath his account whole and sound,
High in heaven he shall be crowned;

Unto which place God bring us all thither,
That we may live body and soul together;
Thereto help the Trinity:
Amen, say ye, for Saint Charity.

FINIS

The Interlude of
John, Tyb, and Sir John

by John Heywood

DRAMATIS PERSONAE

JOHN, THE HUSBAND
TYB, HIS WIFE
SIR JOHN, THE PRIEST

[*At one side of the stage is the principal scene or "station" of the play, the cottage of* JOHN *the husband and* TYB *his wife. There must be trestles and boards for a table and something to represent a fireplace, with a few plain cooking utensils near-by. On the other side of the stage is the more elegant house of* SIR JOHN *the priest, wherein he is seen seated.* JOHN *the husband enters his own house in a great dither and commences to speak.*]

JOHN:

> God speed you, masters, everyone,
> Wot ye not whither my wife is gone?
> I pray God the devil take her!
> For all that I do I cannot make her
> Keep from gadding, when she has the itch,
> Like an Anthony pig, with an old witch,
> Which leads her about hither and thither,
> But, by our Lady, I wot not whither.
> But, by Gog's blood, were she come home,
> Unto this house, by our Lady of Crome,
> I would beat her ere that I drink.
> Beat her, quoth I? yea, until she shall stink!

And at every stroke lay her on the ground
And drag her by the hair round the house around.
I am even mad because I beat her not now.
But I shall repay her strictly, well enow.
There is never a wife between heaven and hell
Who was ever beaten half so well.
            Beaten, quoth I? Yea, but what if she thereof
                die?
Then I may chance to be hanged shortly.
And when I have beaten her till she smokes,
And given her many a hundred strokes,
Think ye that she will amend yet?
Nay, by our Lady, the devil speed wit!
Therefore I will not beat her at all.
            And shall I not beat her? What if I shall?
When she offendeth and doth amiss
And keepeth not her house, as her duty is?
Shall I not beat her, if she do so?
Yes, by Cock's blood, that I shall do.
            But yet I think what my neighbor will say then.
He will say thus, "Whom chidest thou, John, John?"
"Marry!" will I say, "I chide my curst wife,
The veriest drab that ever bare life,
Who doth nothing but go and come,
And I cannot make her keep at home."
Then I think he will say promptly,
"Thwack her coat, John John, and beat her hardly!"
But then unto him my answer shall be,
"The more I beat her, the worse is she;
And worse and worse make her I shall!"
            He will say then, "Beat her not at all."
"And why?" shall I say, "this would be wist.
Is she not mine to chastise as I list?"
            But this is another point worst of all:

Folks will mock me when they hear me brawl.
But, for all that, shall I stop therefore
To chastise my wife ever the more,
And to make her at home for to tarry?
Is not that well done? Yes, by Saint Mary!
That is a sign of an honest man,
For to beat his wife well now and then.

    Therefore I shall beat her, have ye no dread!
And I ought to beat her till she be stark dead.
And why? By God, because it is my pleasure!
And if I should permit her, I swear by God,
Nought should assist me, neither staff nor rod.
In a little while she would be my master.

    Therefore I shall beat her, by Cock's mother,
Both on the one side and on the other,
Before and behind, nought shall be her help,
From the sole of her foot to the top of her skalp.

    But masters, for God's sake, do not intreat
For her when that she shall be beat;
But, for God's passion, let me alone
And I shall thwack her so that she shall groan.
Wherefore I beseech you and heartily you pray,
And I beseech you say me not nay,
But that I may beat her for this once;
And I shall beat her, by Cock's bones,
That she shall stink like a pole-cat!—
But yet, by Gog's body, that need not!
But I shall beat her now without fail;
I shall beat her top and tail,
Head, shoulders, arms, legs and all,
I shall beat her, I trust; that I shall!
And, by Gog's body, I tell you true,
I shall beat her till she be black and blue.

    But where the devil think ye she is gone?

I bet a noble she is with Sir John.
I fear I am beguiled alway;
But yet, in faith, I hope well nay.
Yet I'm almost mad that I never can
See the behavior of our gentlewoman.
And yet, I think, whither as she doth go,
Many an honest wife goeth thither also,
In order to make some pastime and sport.
But then my wife so oft doth thither resort
That I fear she will make me wear a feather.
But yet I need not be afraid either,
For he is her gossip, that is he.
          But abide a while! Yet let me see!
Where the devil hath our gossipry begun?
My wife hath never child, daughter nor son.
          Now if I forbid her to go any more,
Yet will she go as she did before,
Or else will she choose some other place
And then the matter is in as ill case.
          But in faith all these words are in waste,
For I think the matter is done and past.
And when she cometh home she will begin to chide;
But she shall have her payment-stick on her side!
For I shall order her, for all her brawling,
So that she shall repent to go a-caterwauling.
          [TYB, *his wife, overhears him as she stands at
               the door, and abruptly bursts in upon him.*]

TYB:
    Why, whom wilt thou beat, I say, thou knave?
JOHN:
    Who, I, Tyb? None, so God me save.
TYB:
    Yes, I heard thee say thou wouldst someone beat.

JOHN:

    Marry, wife, it was stockfish in Thames Street,

    Which will be good meat during Lent.

    Why, Tyb, what hadst thou thought that I had
      meant?

TYB:

    Marry, methought I heard thee bawling.

    Wilt though never leave this brawling?

    How the devil dost thou thyself behave?

    Shall we always have this work, thou knave?

JOHN:

    What, wife, how sayest thou? was it well guessed by
      me

    That thou wouldest be come home in safety

    As soon as I had kindled a fire?

    Come, warm thee, sweet Tyb, I thee require.

          [He tries hard and clumsily to make a fire.]

TYB:

    O, John, John, I am afraid, by this light,

    That I shall be sore sick this night.

JOHN [*to himself*]:

    By Cock's soul, now I dare bet a swan

    That she comes now straight from Sir John!

    For always when she has fetched from him a lick,

    Then she comes home and says that she is sick.

TYB:

    What sayest thou?

JOHN:

    Marry, I say

    It is meet for a woman to go and play

    Abroad in town for an hour or two.

TYB:

    Well, gentleman, go to, go to!

JOHN:

> Well, let us have no more debate.

TYB [*to herself*]:

> If he do not fight, chide and prate,
> Act as one who were mad, and brawl,
> There is nothing that may please him at all.

JOHN [*to himself*]:

> If that the parish priest, Sir John,
> Did not see her now and then,
> And give her absolution upon a bed,
> From woe and pain she would soon be dead.

TYB:

> For God's sake, John John, do thee not displease;
> Many a time I am ill at ease.
> What thinkest now, am not I somewhat sick?

JOHN [*to himself*]:

> Now would to God and sweet Saint Derrick,
> That thou wert in the water up to thy throat,
> Or in a burning oven red hot,
> To see if I would pull thee out!

TYB:

> Now, John John, to put thee out of doubt,
> Imagine thou where that I was
> Before I came home.

JOHN:

>   My guess,
> Thou wast praying in the church of Paul's
> Upon thy knees for all Christian souls.

TYB:

> Nay.

JOHN:

> Then if thou wast not so holy,
> Show me where thou wast and speak no lie.

TYB:

> Truly, John John, we made a pie,
> I and my gossip Margery,
> And our gossip, the priest, Sir John,
> And my neighbor's youngest daughter, Ann.
> The priest paid for the stuff and the making,
> And Margery, she paid for the baking.

JOHN [*to himself*]:

> By Cock's lily wounds, that same is she
> Who is the greatest bawd from hence to Coventry.

TYB:

> What say you?

JOHN:

> Marry, answer me to this:
> Is not Sir John a good man?

TYB:

> Yes, that he is.

JOHN:

> Ha, Tyb, if I should not grieve thee,
> I have something whereof I would ask thee.

TYB:

> Well, husband, now I think possibly
> Thou art somewhat suspicious of me.
> But, by my soul, I never go to Sir John
> But I find him like an holy man;
> For either he is saying his devotion,
> Or else he is going in procession.

JOHN [*to himself*]:

> Yea, round the bed he goes, I am sure,
> You two together and no more;
> And for to finish the procession,
> He leapeth up and thou liest down.

TYB:

> What sayest thou?

JOHN:

> Marry, I say he doth well;
> For so ought a shepherd to do, as I heard tell,
> For the salvation of all his fold.

TYB:

> John John!

JOHN:

> What is it that thou would?

TYB:

> By my soul, I love thee too true;
> And I shall tell thee, ere I further go,
> The pie that was made, I have it now here,
> And therewith I trust we shall make good cheer.
> > [*She shows him the pie.*]

JOHN:

> By Cock's body, I am very happy.

TYB:

> But knowest thou who gave it?

JOHN:

> What the devil reck I?

TYB:

> By my faith, I shall say true then:
> The devil take me, if it were not Sir John.

JOHN:

> O, hold thy peace, wife, and swear no more!

[*to himself*]:

> But I curse both your hearts therefor.

TYB:

> Yet peradventure thou hast suspicion
> Of that that was never thought nor done.

JOHN:

> Tush, wife, let all such matters be.
> I love thee well, though thou love not me.
> But this pie doth now catch harm;
> Let us set it upon the hearth to warm.

TYB:

Then let us eat it as fast as we can.
But because Sir John is so honest a man,
I would that he should thereof eat his part.

JOHN:

That is reason, I thee assure.

TYB:

Then since that it is thy pleasure,
I pray thee then go to him right,
And pray him come sup with us tonight.

JOHN [to himself]:

Shall he come hither? By Cock's soul, I was accurst,
When that I granted to that word first!
But since I have said it, I dare not say nay,
For then my wife and I should make a fray;
But when he is come, I swear by God's mother,
I would give the devil the one to carry away the
other.

TYB:

What sayest thou?

JOHN:

Marry, he is my curate, I say,
My confessor and my friend alway.
Therefore go thou and seek him immediately
And till thou come again, I will keep the pie.

TYB:

Shall I go for him? Nay, I curse me then!
Go thou, and seek, as fast as thou can,
And tell him it.

JOHN:

Shall I do so?
In faith it is meet for me to go.

TYB:

But thou shalt go tell him, for all that.

JOHN:

>Then shall I tell him, knowest thou what?
>That thou desirest him to come make some cheer.

TYB:

>Nay, that thou desirest him to come sup here.

JOHN:

>Nay, by the cross, wife, thou shalt have the worship
>And the thanks of thy guest who is thy gossip.

TYB [*to herself*]:

>Full oft my husband berates me, I see,
>For this coming of our gentle curate to me.

JOHN:

>What sayest, Tyb? Let me hear that again.

TYB:

>Marry, I perceive very plain
>That thou hast a certain suspicion of Sir John;
>But, by my soul, as I think thereon,
>He is virtuous and full of charity.

JOHN [*to himself*]:

>In faith all the town knoweth better—that he
>Is a whoremonger, a haunter of the stews,
>An hypocrite, a knave whom all men refuse,
>A liar, a wretch, a maker of strife—
>Better than that thou art my good wife.

TYB:

>What is that that thou hast said?

JOHN:

>Marry, I would have the table set and laid
>In this place or that, I care not whither.

TYB:

>Then go to, bring the trestles hither.

JOHN:

>Abide a while, let me put off my gown.
>But yet I am afraid to lay it down,

For I fear it shall be soon stolen.
And yet it may lie safe enough unstolen;
But if I should lay it on the hearth bare,
It might hap to be burned ere I were aware.

> [*He addresses someone in the audience.*]

Therefore I pray you take ye the pain
To keep my gown till I come again.

> [*He snatches it back.*]

But yet he shall not have it, by my fay;
He is so near the door, he might run away.

> [*He addresses someone else in the*
> *audience.*]

But because that ye be trusty and sure,
Ye shall keep it, if it be your pleasure;
And because it is spotted at the skirt,
While ye do nothing, scrape off the dirt.

> [*He speaks to his wife again.*]

Lo, now I am ready to go to Sir John
And bid him come as fast as he can.

TYB:

Yea, do so without any tarrying.—
But I say, hark, thou hast forgot one thing;
Set up the table, and that instantly.

> [JOHN *comes back from the door and puts the*
> *boards on the trestles.*]

Now go thy ways.

JOHN:

I go shortly;
But see your candlesticks be not out of the way.

TYB:

Come again and lay the table, I say.

> [*He comes back and ar-*
> *ranges the table.*]

What! methinks ye have done soon.

JOHN:

> Now I pray God that his malediction
> Light on my wife and on the bald priest.

TYB:

> Now go thy ways and hie thee, seest?

JOHN:

> I pray to Christ, if my wish be no sin,
> That the priest may break his neck when he comes
>   in.

TYB:

> Now come again.

JOHN:

> What a mischief wilt thou, fool?

TYB:

> Marry, I say, bring hither yonder stool.

JOHN:

> ,Now go to! A little would make me
> For to say thus, a vengeance take thee!

> > *[He brings the stool.]*

TYB:

> Now go to him and tell him plain
> That till thou bring him thou wilt not come again.

JOHN:

> This pie doth burn here as it doth stand.

TYB:

> Go wash me these two cups in my hand.

> > *[He washes the two cups.]*

JOHN:

> I go—with a mischief light on thy face!

TYB:

> Go and bid him hie him apace;
> And the while I shall all things amend.

JOHN:

> This pie burneth here at this end.
> Understandest thou?

TYB:

Go thy ways, I say!

JOHN:

I will go now as fast as I may.

TYB:

Stop! Come once again; I had forgot.
Look if there be any ale in the pot.

JOHN:

Now a vengeance and eternal strife
Light on the bald priest and on my wife,
On the pot, the ale and on the table,
The candle, the pie and all the rabble,
On the trestles and on the stool!
It is much ado to please a curst fool.

[He fills the alepot.]

TYB:

Go thy ways now and tarry no more,
For I am a-hungered very sore.

JOHN:

Marry, I go.

TYB:

But come once again yet!
Bring hither that bread, lest I forget.

[He brings the bread.]

JOHN:

Truly, it is time to turn
The pie, for truly, it doth burn.

TYB:

Lord, how my husband now doth patter
And of the pie still doth clatter.
Go now, and bid him come this way;
I have bid thee an hundred times today.

JOHN:

I will not give a straw, I tell you plain,
If that the pie grow cold again.

TYB:

What! art thou not gone yet out of this place?
I had thought thou hadst been come again in this
    space.
But, by Cock's soul, if I should do thee right,
I should break thy knave's head tonight.

JOHN:

Nay then, if my wife be set a-chiding,
It is time for me to go at her bidding.
There is a proverb, as true as I'm alive:
"He must needs walk whom the devil drives."
        [*He crosses the stage to the Priest's house.*]
Good day, Master Curate, may I come in
At your chamber door without any sin?

SIR JOHN:

Who is there now who would see me?
What! John John! What news with thee?

JOHN:

Marry, Sir, to tell you shortly,
My wife and I pray you heartily,
And both desire you with all our might
That ye would come and sup with us tonight.

SIR JOHN:

Ye must pardon me; in faith I cannot.

JOHN:

Yes, I desire you, good Sir John,
Trouble yourself this once. And yet, at the least,
If ye will do nought at my request,
Yet do something for the love of my wife.

SIR JOHN:

I will not go, lest it gender strife.
But I shall tell thee what thou shalt do;
Thou shalt tarry and sup with me ere thou go.

JOHN:

>Will ye not go then? Why so?
>I pray you tell me, is there any disdain
>Or any enmity between you twain?

SIR JOHN:

>In faith, to tell thee, between thee and me,
>She is as prudent a woman as any may be.
>I know it well; for I have had the charge
>Of her soul and searched her conscience at large.
>I never knew her but honest and wise,
>Without any evil or any vice,
>Save one fault—I know in her no more—
>And because I rebuke her now and then therefor,
>She is angry with me and hath me in hate.
>And yet whatever I do, I do it for your wealth.

JOHN:

>Now God reward you, good Master Curate,
>And as ye do, so send you your health.
>Indeed, I am bound to you for a pleasure.

SIR JOHN:

>Yet thou thinkest amiss, peradventure,
>That of her body she should not be a good woman.
>But I shall tell thee what I have done, John,
>In that matter. She and I are sometimes aloft,
>And I belie her many a time and oft
>Just to prove her; yet I could never espy
>That ever anyone did worse with her than I.

JOHN:

>Sir, that is the least care I have of nine,
>Thanked be God and your good doctrine.
>But, if it please you, tell me the matter,
>And the quarrel between you and her.

SIR JOHN:

>I shall tell thee; but thou must keep secrecy.

JOHN:
> As for that, Sir, I promise faithfully.

SIR JOHN:
> I shall tell thee now the matter plain:
> She is angry with me and hath me in disdain,
> Inasmuch as I do her oft entice,
> To do some penance by my advice,
> Since she will never leave her squalling
> But always with thee she is chiding and brawling.
> And therefore, I know, she hateth my presence.

JOHN:
> Nay, in good faith, saving your reverence!

SIR JOHN:
> I know very well she hath me in hate.

JOHN:
> Nay, I dare swear for her, Master Curate.

[*aside*]:
> But, was I not a very knave?
> I thought surely, so God me save,
> That he had loved my wife to deceive me.
> And now he freeth himself; and here I see
> He doth as much as he can, for his life,
> To stop the struggle between me and my wife.

SIR JOHN:
> If ever she did or thought me any ill,
> Now I forgive her with my free will.
> Therefore, John John, now get thee home,
> And thank thy wife and say I will not come.

JOHN:
> Yet let me know now, good Sir John,
> Where ye will go to supper then.

SIR JOHN:
> I care not greatly if I tell thee.
> On Saturday last I and two or three

Of my friends made an appointment
And against this night we did assent
That in a place we would sup together.
And one of them said she would bring thither
Ale and bread; and for my part, I
Said that I would give them a pie.
And there I gave them money for the making.
And another said she would pay for the baking.
And so we purpose to make good cheer
For to drive away care and thought.

JOHN:

Then I pray you, Sir, tell me here
Whither should all these things be brought?

SIR JOHN:

By my faith, if I should not lie,
It should be delivered to thy wife, the pie.

JOHN:

By God! it is at my house, standing by the fire.

SIR JOHN:

Who ordered that pie? I thee inquire.

JOHN:

By my faith, and I shall not lie,
It was my wife and her gossip Margery,
And your good worship called Sir John,
And my neighbor's youngest daughter, Ann.
Your worship paid for the stuff and making
And Margery, she paid for the baking.

SIR JOHN:

If thou wilt have me now, in faith, I will go.

JOHN:

Marry, I beseech your worship do so.
My wife tarrieth for none but us twain;
She thinketh long ere I come again.

SIR JOHN:

Well now, if she chide me in thy presence,
I will be content and take it in patience.

JOHN:

By Cock's soul, if she once chide,
Or frown, or lour, or look aside,
I shall bring you a staff, as large as I may have;
Then beat her, and spare not! I give you good leave
To chastise her for her wicked quarreling.

[*They go back to* JOHN'S *house.*]

TYB:

The devil take thee for thy long tarrying!
Here is not a drop of water, by my gown,
To wash our hands before we sit down.
Go, and hie thee as fast as a snail,
And with fresh water fill me this pail.

JOHN:

I thank our Lord for his good grace
That I cannot rest long in one place!

TYB:

Go, fetch water, I say, at a word,
For it is time the pie were on the board.
And go with a vengeance and say thou art prayed.

SIR JOHN:

Ah, good gossip, is that well said?

TYB:

Welcome, mine own sweet heart!
We shall make some cheer ere we depart.

JOHN:

Cock's soul, look how he approacheth near
Unto my wife! This abateth my cheer.

[JOHN *goes out with the pail.*]

SIR JOHN:

By God, I would ye had heard the toys,
The trifles, the mocks, the fables and decoys,

That I made thy husband to believe and think!
Thou mightest as well into the earth sink,
As thou couldest forbear laughing any while.

TYB:

I pray thee, let me hear part of that wile.

SIR JOHN:

Marry, I shall tell thee as fast as I can—
But peace! No more! Yonder cometh thy good man.
> [JOHN *returns with the pail leaking.*]

JOHN:

Cock's soul, what have we here?
As far as I saw, he drew very near
Unto my wife.

TYB:

What, art come so soon?
Give us water to wash now. Have done.

JOHN:

By Cock's soul, it was even now full to the brink,
But it was out again ere I could think.
Whereof I marveled, by God's great might,
And then I looked between me and the light,
And I spied a cleft both large and wide,
Lo, wife, here it is on one side.

TYB:

Why dost not stop it?

JOHN:

Why, how should I do it?

TYB:

Take a little wax.

JOHN:

How shall I come to it?

SIR JOHN:

Marry, here be two wax candles, I say,
Which my gossip Margery gave me yesterday.

TYB:

>Tush, let him alone; for, by the Rood,
>It is a pity to help him or do him good.

SIR JOHN:

>What, John John, canst thou make no shift?
>Take this wax and stop therewith the clift.

JOHN:

>This wax is as hard as any wire.

TYB:

>Thou must chafe it a little at the fire.

JOHN:

>She who bought thee these wax candles twain,
>She is a good companion certain!

>>[JOHN *goes to the hearth to mend the pail.*]

TYB:

>What, was it not my gossip Margery?

SIR JOHN:

>Yes; she is a blessed woman, surely.

TYB:

>Now would God I were as good as she,
>For she is virtuous and full of charity.

JOHN [*to himself*]:

>Now so God help me, and by my halidom,
>She is the arrantest bawd between here and Rome.

TYB:

>What sayest?

JOHN:

>>Marry, I chafe the wax,
>And I chafe it so hard that my finger cracks.
>But take up this pie that I here turn.
>If it stand long, in truth, it will burn.

TYB:

>Yea, but thou must chafe the wax, I say.

>>[JOHN *approaches the table.*]

JOHN:

Bid him sit down, I thee pray—
Sit down, good Sir John, I you require.

TYB:

Go, I say, and chafe the wax by the fire
While that we sup, Sir John and I.

JOHN:

And how now? what will ye do with the pie?
Shall I not eat thereof a morsel?

TYB:

Go, and chafe the wax while thou art well,
And let us have no more prating thus.

[SIR JOHN *commences to say grace.*]

SIR JOHN:

Benedicte—

JOHN:

Dominus.

TYB:

Now go chafe the wax, with a mischief!

JOHN:

What! I come to bless the board, sweet wife.
It is my custom now and then.
Much good do it you, Master Sir John!

TYB:

Go chafe the wax and here no longer tarry.

JOHN [*to himself at the fire*]:

And is not this a very purgatory,
To see folks eat, and one may not eat a bit?
By Cock's soul, I am a very woodcock.
This pail here, now a vengeance take it!
Now my wife giveth me a proud mock!

TYB:

What dost?

JOHN:

Marry, I chafe the wax here,
And I imagine to make you good cheer.—

[*aside*]:

That a vengeance take you both as ye sit,
For I know well I shall not eat a bit.
But yet, in faith, if I might eat one morsel,
I would think the matter went very well.

SIR JOHN [*eating at the table*]:

Gossip John John, now much good do it you,
What cheer make you, there by the fire?

JOHN:

Master Parson, I thank you now,
I fare well enow after mine own desire.

SIR JOHN:

What dost, John John, I thee require?

JOHN:

I chafe the wax here by the fire.

TYB:

Here is good drink and here is a good pie!

SIR JOHN:

We fare very well, thanked be our Lady!

TYB:

Look how the cuckold chafeth the wax that is hard,
And, for his life, dareth not look hitherward.

SIR JOHN [*to* JOHN]:

What doth my gossip?

JOHN:

I chafe the wax—

[*aside*]:

And I chafe it so hard that my finger cracks.
Also the smoke putteth out my eyes two;
I burn my face and soil my clothes also,

And yet I dare not say one word;
And they sit laughing yonder at the board.

TYB:

Now, by my troth, it is a pretty jape
For a wife to make her husband her ape.
Look at John John, who makes hard shift
To chafe the wax, to stop therewith the clift!

JOHN [*to himself*]:

Yea, would that a vengeance took ye both two,
Both him and thee, and thee and him, also!
And that ye may choke with the same meat
At the first morsel that ye do eat.

TYB:

Of what thing now dost thou clatter,
John John! or whereof dost thou patter?

JOHN:

I chafe the wax and make hard shift
To stop herewith of the pail the rift.

SIR JOHN:

So must he do, John John, by my father's kin,
Who is bound of wedlock in the yoke.

JOHN [*to himself*]:

Look how the bald priest crammeth in!
Oh would to God he might therewith choke!

TYB:

Now Master Parson, pleaseth your goodness,
To tell us some tale of mirth or sadness,
For our pastime in way of communication?

SIR JOHN:

I am content to do it for your recreation;
And of three miracles I shall to you say.

JOHN:

What! must I chafe the wax all day,
And stand here roasting by the fire?

SIR JOHN:

>Thou must do somewhat at thy wife's desire.
>I know a man who wedded had a wife—
>As fair a woman as ever bear life—
>And within a week thereafter, right soon,
>He went beyond sea and left her alone,
>And tarried there about seven year.
>And as he came homeward he had a heavy cheer,
>For it was told that she was in heaven.
>But when that he travelled home again was,
>He found his wife, and with her children seven,
>Which she had had in the mean space—
>Yet had she not had so many by three,
>If she had not had the help of me.
>Is not this a miracle, if ever there were any,
>That this good wife should have children so many
>Here in this town, while her husband should be
>In a far country beyond the sea?

JOHN [aside]:

>Now, in good sooth, this is a wondrous miracle!
>But for your labor, I would that your tackle
>Were in a scalding water well sod.

TYB:

>Peace, I say; thou hinderest the word of God.

SIR JOHN:

>Another miracle also I shall you say,
>Of a woman who that many a day
>Had been wedded, and in all that season
>She had no child, neither daughter nor son.
>Wherefore to Saint Modwin she went on pil-
>   grimage,
>And offered there a live pig, as is the usage
>Of the wives who in London dwell;
>And through the virtue thereof, truly to tell,

Within a month after, right shortly,
She was delivered of a child as large as I.
How say you, is not this a miracle wonderous?

JOHN:

Yes, in good sooth, Sir, it is marvelous.
But surely, according to my opinion,
That child was neither daughter nor son.
For certainly, if I be not beguiled,
She was delivered of a knave child.

TYB:

Peace, I say, for God's passion!
Thou hinderest Sir John's communication.

SIR JOHN:

The third miracle also is this:
I knew another woman also, ywis,
Who was wedded, and within five months after
She was delivered of a fair daughter,
As well formed in every member and joint,
And as perfect in every point,
As though she had gone five months, full to the end.
Lo! here is five months of advantage!

JOHN:

A wonderous miracle, so God me amend!
I would each wife who is bound in marriage,
And who is wedded here within this place,
Might have as quick speed in every such case.

TYB:

Forsooth, Sir John, yet for all that,
I have seen the day that Puss, my cat,
Hath had in a year kittens eighteen.

JOHN:

Yea, Tyb my wife, and that have I seen.
But how say you, Sir John, was it good, your pie?
The devil a morsel thereof ate I.

By the good Lord, this is a pitiful work.
But now I see well the old proverb is true:
"The parish priest forgetteth he ever was clerk."
But, Sir John, doth it not remind you,
How I was your clerk and helped you mass to sing,
And held the basin always at the offering?
Ye never had half so good a clerk as I:
But, notwithstanding all this, now our pie
Is eaten up; there is not left a bit;
And you two together there do sit,
Eating and drinking at your desire,
And I am John John, who must stand by the fire
Chafing the wax and dare none other wise do.

SIR JOHN:

And shall we always sit here still, we two?
That were too much.

TYB:

Then rise we from this place.

SIR JOHN:

And kiss me then in the stead of grace.
And farewell, sweetheart, and my love so dear!

JOHN:

Cock's body, this wax has waxed cold again here.
But say, shall I go anon to bed,
And eat nothing, neither meat nor bread?
I have not been used to have such fare.

TYB:

Why, were ye not served there as ye are,
Chafing the wax, standing by the fire?

JOHN:

Why, what meat gave ye me, I you require?

SIR JOHN:

Wast thou not served, I pray thee, heartily,
Both with the bread, the ale and the pie?

JOHN:

    No, Sir, I had none of that fare.

TYB:

    Why, were ye not served there as ye are,

    Standing by the fire, chafing the wax?

JOHN [*to himself*]:

    Lo, here be many trifles and knacks;

    By Cock's soul, they think I am either drunk or mad!

TYB:

    And no meat, John John, have ye had?

JOHN:

    No, Tyb my wife, I had not a whit.

TYB:

    What, not a morsel?

JOHN:

          No, not a bit.

    From hunger, I believe, I shall fall in a swoon.

SIR JOHN:

    Oh, that were a pity, I swear by my crown.

TYB:

    But is it true?

JOHN:

          Yea, for a surety.

TYB:

    Dost thou lie?

JOHN:

          No, so God help me!

TYB:

    Hast thou had nothing?

JOHN:

          No, not a bit.

TYB:

    Hast thou not drunk?

JOHN:
> No, not a whit.

TYB:
> Where wast thou?

JOHN:
> By the fire I did stand.

TYB:
> What didest?

JOHN:
> I chafed this wax in my hand,
> While I knew of wedded men the pain
> That they have, and yet dare not complain;
> For the smoke put out my eyes two,
> I burned my face, and soiled my clothes also,
> Mending the pail, which is so rotten and old,
> That it will scarcely together hold.
> And since it is so, and since that ye twain
> Would give me no meat for my sustenance,
> By Cock's soul, I will stand no further pain,
> Ye shall do all yourselves, with a very vengeance,
> For me! And take thou there thy pail now,
> And if thou canst mend it, let me see how.
> > [*He throws the pail at them.*]

TYB:
> Ah, whoreson knave, hast thou broke my pail?
> Thou shalt repent, by Cock's lily nail!
> Reach me my distaff or my clipping shears!
> I shall make the blood run about his ears.

JOHN:
> Nay, stand still, drab, I say, and come not near;
> For, by Cock's blood, if thou come here,
> Or if thou once stir toward this place,
> I shall throw this shovel full of coals in thy face.

TYB:

    You whoreson drivel! get thee out of my door!

JOHN:

    Nay, get thou out of my house, thou priest's whore!

SIR JOHN:

    Thou liest, whoreson cuckold, even to thy face!

JOHN:

    And thou liest, bald priest, with an evil grace!

TYB:

    And thou liest!

JOHN:

            And thou liest!

SIR JOHN:

              And thou liest again.

JOHN:

    By Cock's soul, whoreson priest, thou shalt be slain.

    Thou hast eaten our pie and given me nought.

    By Cock's blood, it shall be full dearly bought!

TYB:

    At him, Sir John, or else God give thee sorrow!

JOHN:

    And have at you, whore and thief, Saint George to

      borrow!

        [They fight and pull each other by the ears

        for a while, and finally the Priest and the

        Wife go out.]

JOHN:

    Ah, sirs, I have paid some of them even as I list.

    They have born many a blow with my fist.

    I thank God, I have welted them well,

    And driven them hence. But yet, can ye tell

    Whither they are gone? For, by God, I fear me

    That they be gone together, he and she,

Unto his chamber; and perhaps she will,
In spite of my valor, tarry there still;
And peradventure, there he and she
Will make me cuckold, even to anger me.
And then had I a pig in the worse pannier.
Therefore, by God, I will hie me thither
To see if they do me any villainy.
And thus, farewell, this noble company!

[JOHN *hurries out and the play ends.*]

The Interlude of
The Pardoner and the Friar

by John Heywood

DRAMATIS PERSONAE

THE FRIAR
THE PARDONER
THE PARSON
PRATT, THE CONSTABLE

[*The scene is a church; the audience at the play represents the congregation.* A FRIAR *enters and commences to address them.*]

FRIAR:

> *Deus hic,* the Holy Trinity,
> Preserve all that now here be!
> Dear brethren, if you will consider
> The cause, why I am come hither,
> Ye would be glad to know my intent;
> For I come not hither for money nor for rent,
> I come not hither for meat nor for meal,
> But I come hither for your soul's heal:
> I come not hither to poll nor to shave,
> I come not hither to beg nor to crave,
> I come not hither to gloss nor to flatter,
> I come not hither to babble nor to clatter,
> I come not hither to fable nor to lie,
> But I come hither your souls to edify.

For we friars are bound the people to teach,
The gospel of Christ openly to preach,
As did the apostles by Christ their master sent,
To turn the people and make them to repent.
But since the apostles from heaven would not come,
We friars now must occupy their room,
We friars are bound to search men's conscience,
We may not care for groats nor for pence,
We friars have professed wilful poverty,
No penny in our purse have may we;
Knife nor staff may we none carry,
Except we should from the gospel vary.
For worldly adversity may we be in no sorrow,
We may not care today for our meat tomorrow,
Barefoot and barelegged must we go also;
We may not care for frost nor snow;
We may have no manner care, nor think
Neither for our meat nor for our drink;
But let our thoughts from such things be as free
As be the birds that in the air flee.
Because Our Lord, named sweet Jesus,
In the gospel speaketh to us thus:
"Through all the world go ye," saith He,
"And to every creature speak ye of Me;
And show of My doctrine and cunning,
And that they may be glad of your coming.
If that you enter in any house anywhere,
Look that ye salute them and bid My peace be there;
And if that house be worthy and elect,
The same peace there then shall take effect;
And if that house be cursed or pervert,
The same peace then shall to yourself revert.
And furthermore, if any such there be
Who do deny for to receive ye,

And do despise your doctrine and your lore,
At such a house tarry ye no more;
And from your shoes scrape away the dust
To their reproof; and I, both true and just,
Shall vengeance take for their sinful deed."
Wherefore, my friends, to this text take heed:
Beware how ye despise the poor friars,
Which are in this world Christ's ministers;
But do them with an hearty cheer receive,
Lest they happen your houses for to leave;
And then God will take vengeance in His ire.
Wherefore I now, that am a poor friar,
Did inquire where any people were
Which were disposed the word of God to hear;
And as I came hither, one did me tell
That in this town right good folk did dwell,
Which to hear the Word of God would be glad;
And as soon as I thereof knowledge had,
I hither hied me as fast as I might,
Directed indeed by God's grace and might,
And by your patient cooperation
Here to make a simple collation;
Wherefore I require all you in this presence
For to abide and give due audience.
But, first of all
Now here I shall
To God my prayer make,
To give you grace
All in this place
His doctrine for to take.

> [*Here* THE FRIAR *kneels down, saying his pray-
> ers, and meanwhile* THE PARDONER *enters
> carrying a load of relics, to declare what
> each of them is and their great power and
> virtue.*]

PARDONER:

God and Saint Leonard send you all his grace,
As many as are assembled in this place!
Good devout people that here do assemble,
I pray God that ye may all well resemble
The image after which you are wrought,
And that ye save what Christ in you bought.
Devout Christian people, I shall make it clear
How I am come to visit you here.
Wherefore let us pray thus, ere I begin:
Our Saviour preserve you all from sin,
And enable you to receive this blessed pardon,
Which is the greatest under the sun:
Granted by the Pope in his bulls under lead,
Which pardon ye shall find when ye are dead,
Who offereth either groats or else pence
To these holy relics which, ere I go hence,
I shall here show in open audience,
Exhorting ye all to do them reverence.
But first ye shall know well that I come from Rome;
Lo, here my bulls, all and some;
Our liege Lord's seal here on my patent
I bear with me my body to warrant;
That no man be so bold, be he priest or clerk,
Me to disturb in Christ's holy work;
Nor have no disdain nor yet scorn
Of these holy relics which saints have worn.
First here I show ye of an holy Jew's hip
A bone—I pray you, take good keep
To my words and mark them well:
If any of your beasts' bellies do swell,
Dip this bone in the water that he doth take
Into his body, and the swellings shall slake;
And if any worm have your beasts stung,
Take of this water, and wash his tongue,

And it will be whole anon; and furthermore
Of pox and scabs and every sore
He shall be quite whole that drinketh of this well
That this bone is dipped in: it is truth that I tell.
And if any man, that any beast owneth,
Once in the week, ere that the cock croweth,
Fasting will drink of this well a draught,
As that holy Jew hath us taught,
His beasts and his stores shall multiply.
And, masters all, it helpeth well,
Though a man be foul in jealous rage,
Let a man with this water make his pottage,
He shall mistrust his wife no more,
Even though he knew her fault before,
Or had been taken with friars, two or three.
Here is a mitten, too, as ye may see,
He that his hand will put in this mitten,
He shall have increase of his grain,
That he has sown, be it wheat or oats,
So that he offer pence or else groats.
And another holy relic here see ye may:
The blessed arm of sweet Saint Sunday;
And whosoever is blessed with this right hand,
Cannot speed amiss by sea nor by land.
And if he offereth with good devotion,
He shall not fail to come to high promotion.
And another holy relic here may ye see:
The great toe of the Holy Trinity;
And whosoever once doth it in his mouth take,
He shall never be diseased with the toothache;
Cancer nor pox shall there none breed:
This that I show you is matter indeed.
And here is of our lady a relic full good:
Her veil which she wore with her French hood,

When she went out and shunned sun-burning.
Women with child who be in mourning
By virtue thereof shall be soon eased,
And from their travail full soon also released,
And if this veil they do devoutly kiss,
And offer thereto, as their devotion is.
Here is another relic also, a precious one,
Of All-Hallows the blessed jaw bone,
Which relic without any fail
Against poison chiefly doth prevail;
For whomsoever it toucheth without doubt,
All manner venom from him shall issue out,
So that it shall hurt no manner wight.
Lo, of this relic the great power and might,
Which preserveth from poison every man!
Lo, of Saint Michael also the brain-pan,
Which for the headache is a preservative
To every man or beast that beareth life;
And further it shall stand him in better stead,
For his head shall never ache when that he is dead,
Nor he shall feel no manner grief nor pain,
Though with a sword one cleave it then a-twain;
But be as one that lay in a dead sleep.
Wherefore to these relics now come crouch and
    creep,
But look that ye offering to them make,
Or else can ye no manner profit take.
But one thing, ye women all, I warrant you:
If any one be in this place now,
That hath done sin so horrible that she
Dare not for shame thereof shriven be,
Or any woman, be she young or old,
That hath made her husband cuckold:
Such folk shall have no power nor no grace
To offer to my relics in this place;

And whoso findeth herself out of such blame,
Come hither to me, on Christ's holy name,
And because ye
Shall unto me
Give credence at the full
Mine authority
Now shall ye see,
Lo, here the Pope's bull!

> [THE FRIAR *begins his sermon, and at the same
> time* THE PARDONER *displays his bulls and
> authorities from Rome. Consequently the
> two following speeches must be imagined as
> spoken simultaneously.*]

FRIAR:

Date et dabitur vobis,
Good devout people, this place of scripture
Is to you that have not literature—
Is to say in our English tongue,
If you part your goods the poor folk among,
God shall then give unto you again;
This is the gospel, that is written plain.
Therefore give your alms in the freest wise,
Keep not your goods. Fye, fye on covetise!
That sin with God is most abominable,
And is also the sin that is most damnable.
In Scripture also I remark, sirs, how
—What a babbling maketh yonder fellow—
In scripture also is there many a place
Which showeth that many a man so greatly lacketh
    grace,
That when to them God hath abundance sent,
They would distribute none to the indigent,
Whereat God, having great indignation,
Punished these men after a divers fashion,

As the gospel full nobly doth declare
How the rich man Epulus reigning in welfare,
And on his board dishes delicate—
Poor Lazarus came begging at his gate,
Desiring some food his hunger to relieve,
But the rich man nothing would him give,
Not so much as a few crumbs of bread,
Wherefore poor Lazarus of famine straight was
      dead
And angels his soul to heaven did carry;
But now the rich man, on the contrary,
When he was dead, went to misery and pain.
Wherefore evermore he shall remain
In blazing fire, which shall never cease.—
But I say, thou Pardoner, I bid thee hold thy peace!
What, standest thou there all the day smattering?

PARDONER:

Worshipful masters, ye shall understand
That Pope Leo the Tenth hath granted with his
      hand,
And by his bulls confirmed under lead
To all manner of people both quick and dead,
Ten thousand years and as many Lents of pardon
When they are dead, their souls to guerdon,
Who will with their penny or almsdeed
Put their hands to the good speed
Of the holy chapel of sweet Saint Leonard,
Which late by fire was destroyed and marred.—
Ay, by the mass, one cannot hear
For the babbling of yonder foolish friar.—
And also, masters, as I was about to tell,
Pope Julius the Sixth hath granted fair and well,
And doth twelve thousand years of pardon to them
      send,
That aught to this holy chapel lend.

Pope Boniface the Ninth also,
Pope Julius, Pope Innocent, with divers popes mo',
Have granted to the sustaining of the same
Five thousand years of pardon to each of you by
    name,
And clean remission also of their sin,
As oftentimes as you put in
Any money into the Pardoner's coffer,
Or any money up unto it offer;
Or he that offereth penny or groat,
Or he that giveth the Pardoner a new coat,
Or takes from me either image or letter,
Whereby this poor chapel may fare the better.
And, God wot, it is a full gracious deed
For which God shall requite you well your meed.
Now help our poor chapel, if it be your will.—
And I say, thou Friar, hold thy tongue still!
Marry, why standest thou there all the day clatter-
    ing?

FRIAR:

Marry, fellow, I come hither to preach the Word of
    God,
Which of no man may be forbode;
But heard with silence and good intent,
And why? It maketh evident
The very way and path that shall them lead
Even to heaven's gates, as straight as any thread.
He that hindereth the Word of God from audience,
Standeth accursed in the great sentence,
And so art thou for interrupting me.

PARDONER:

Nay, thou art a cursed knave, and that shalt thou
    see;
And all such that to me make interruption,
The Pope sends them excommunication

By his bulls here ready to be read,
By bishops and his cardinals confirmed.
And so if thou disturb me in any thing,
Thou art also a traitor to the king.
For here hath he granted me under his broad seal,
That no man, if he love his weal,
Should me disturb or stop in any wise;
And if thou dost the king's commandment despise,
I shall make thee be set fast by the feet,
And, where thou saidst that thou art more meet
Among the people here for to preach,
Because thou dost them the very way teach,
How to come to heaven above,
Therein thou liest, and that shall I prove,
And by good reason I shall make thee bow,
And know that I am meeter than art thou.
For thou, when thou hast taught them once the way,
Thou carest not whether they come there, yea or
    nay;
But when that thou hast done altogether,
And taught them the way for to come hither,
Yet all that thou canst imagine
Is but to use virtue and abstain from sin.
And if they fall once, then thou canst no more;
Thou canst not give them a salve for their sore.
But these my letters be clean purgation,
Although never so many sins they have done.
But when thou hast taught them the way and all,
Yet, ere they come there, they may have many a fall
In the way, ere that they come thither,
And why? The way to heaven is very slidder.
But I will teach them after another rate,
For I shall bring them to heaven's gate,

And be their guide, and conduct all things,
And lead them thither by the purse-strings.
So that they shall not fall, although they would.

FRIAR:

Hold thy peace, knave, thou art very bold.
Thou pratest, in faith, even like a Pardoner.

PARDONER:

Why despisest thou the Pope's minister?
Masters, here I curse him openly,
And therewith warn all this whole company
By the Pope's great authority,
That ye leave him and harken unto me.
For till he be assoiled his words take no effect,
For out of Holy Church he is now clean reject.

FRIAR:

My masters, he doth but jest and rave;
It matters not for the words of a knave;
But to the word of God do reverence
And hear me forth with due audience.
Masters, I showed you ere while of almsdeed—

[*At this point* THE PARDONER *again inter-
rupts, and the next two speeches are again
to be imagined as spoken simultaneously.*]

PARDONER:

Masters, this pardon which I showed you before
Is the greatest that ever was since God was bore;
Because without confession or contrition,
By this shall ye have clean remission
And be forgiven of the sins seven.
Come to this pardon, if ye will come to heaven.
Come to this pardon, if ye will be in bliss.
This is the pardon which ye cannot miss.
This is the pardon which shall men's souls win,
This is the pardon, the ridder of your sin,

This is the pardon that purchaseth all grace,
This is the pardon for all manner of trespass,
This is the pardon from which all mercy doth
    spring,
This is the pardon that to heaven shall ye bring.—

FRIAR:

Masters, I showed you ere while of almsdeed
And how ye should give poor folks at their need;
And if of your goods that thing once were done,
Doubt not that God should give you retribution.
But now further it ought to be declared
Who be these poor folk that should have your
    reward,
Who be these poor folk of whom I speak and name?
Certes, we poor friars are the same.
We friars daily take pain, I say,
We friars daily do both fast and pray,
We friars travail and labor every hour,
We friars take pain for the love of our Savior,
We friars also go on limitation
For to preach to every Christian nation.—
But I say, thou Pardoner, wilt thou keep silence
    soon?

PARDONER:

Yea, it is like to be, when I have done!

FRIAR:

Marry, therefore the more knave art thou, I say,
That perturbest the Word of God, I say;
For neither thyself will hear God's doctrine,
Nor suffer others their ears to incline.
Wherefore our Savior, in his holy Scripture,
Giveth thee thy judgment, thou cursed creature,
Speaking to thee after this manner:
Maledictus qui audit verbum Dei negligenter—

Woe be that man, saith our Lord, that giveth no
  audience,
Or heareth the Word of God with negligence.

PARDONER:

Now thou hast spoken all, sir daw,
I care not for thee an old straw;
I had liever thou were hanged up with a rope,
Than I, who am come from the Pope,
And thereby God's minister, while thou standest and
  prate,
Should be fain to knock without the gate.
Therefore preach directly thy bellyful,
But I nevertheless will declare the Pope's bull.

> [*Once more the two men address the congre-
> gation at the same time, and the two fol-
> lowing speeches are to be understood as
> spoken simultaneously.*]

FRIAR:

Now, my friends, I have afore showed ye
That it is good to give your charity,
And further I have at length to you told
Who be these people that ye receive should,
That is to say, us friars poor,
Who for our living must beg from door to door,
For of our own private goods we have no private
  thing,
But what we get of devout people's giving;
And in our place be friars three score and three
Which only live on men's charity.
For we friars wilful charity profess,
We may have no money either more or less;
For worldly treasure we may nought care;
Our souls must be rich and our bodies bare.
And one thing I had almost left behind,
Which before came not to my mind.

And doubtless it is none other thing
But when you will give your alms and offering,
Look that ye distribute it wisely,
Not to every man that for it will cry;
For if ye give your alms in that wise,
It shall not both to them and us suffice.—

PARDONER:

Now, my masters, as I have afore declared
That pardoners from you may not be spared,
Now hereafter shall follow and ensue
That followeth of pardons the great virtue.
We pardoners for your souls be as necessary
As is the meat for our bodies hungry;
For pardon is the thing that bringeth men to heaven;
Pardon delivereth them from the sins seven;
Pardon for every crime may dispense;
Pardon purchaseth grace for all offence;
Yea, though ye had slain both father and mother.
And this pardon is chief above all other.
For who to it offereth groat or penny,
Though sins he had done never so many,
And though that he had all his kindred slain,
This pardon shall rid them from everlasting pain.
There is no sin so abominable
Which to remit this pardon is not able,
As well declareth the meaning of this letter.
Ye cannot, therefore, bestow your money better.
Let us not here stand idle all the day;
Give us some money, ere that we go away.

FRIAR:

But I say, thou lewd fellow, thou,
Had you no other time to show your bulls but now?
Canst not tarry and abide till soon,
And read them then, when preaching is done?

PARDONER:

    I will read them now, what sayest thou thereto?

    Hast thou anything therewith to do?

    Thinkest that I will stand and tarry for thy leisure?

    Am I bound to do so much for thy pleasure?

FRIAR:

    For my pleasure? nay I would thou knowest it well:

    It becometh the knave never a deal

    To prate thus boldly in my presence,

    Checking the Word of God of audience.

PARDONER:

    Checking the Word of God, quod a? nay let the
        whoreson drivel

    Prate here all day, with a foul evil,

    And all thy sermon goeth on covetise,

    And biddest men beware of avarice;

    And yet in thy sermon dost thou none other thing,

    But for alms stand all the day begging!

FRIAR:

    Leave thy railing, I would thee advise—

PARDONER:

    Nay, leave thou thy babbling, if thou be wise—

FRIAR:

    I would thou knowest it, knave, I will not leave a
        whit—

PARDONER:

    No more will I, I do thee well to wit—

FRIAR:

    It is not thou shall make me hold my peace—

PARDONER:

    Then speak on directly, if thou thinkest it for thy
        ease—

FRIAR:

    For I will speak, whether thou wilt or no—

PARDONER:

    In faith I care not, for I will speak also—

FRIAR:

    Wherefore directly let us both go to—

PARDONER:

    See which shall be better heard of us two—

> [*The two succeeding speeches, as in the earlier
> instances, are spoken simultaneously.*]

FRIAR:

    What, should ye give aught to prating pardoners,
    What, should ye give aught to these bold beggars,
    Let them honestly labor for their living.
    They are much hurt by good men's giving.
    For that maketh them idle and slothful to work,
    Careless of all things and given to shirk;
    They would go directly both to plough and cart,
    If they should once feel necessity's smart.
    But we friars are not in like estate,
    For our hands with such things we may not maculate.
    We friars are not in like condition;
    We may have no prebends nor commission;
    Of all temporal service are we forbode,
    And only bound to the service of God,
    And therewith to pray for every Christian nation,
    That God vouchsafe to save them from damnation.
    But some of you are so hard of heart,
    Ye cannot weep, though ye full sore smart.
    Wherefore some man must ye hire for your needs
    Who must intreat God for your misdeeds.
    Ye can hire no better, in mine opinion,
    Than us, God's servants, men of religion.
    And specially God heareth us poor friars
    And is attentive unto our desires,

For the more of religion, the more heard by our
   Lord.
And that it should be so, good reason doth accord.
Therefore doubt not masters, I am even he
To whom ye should part with your charity.
We friars be they who should your alms take
Who for your souls' health do both watch and wake.
We friars pray, God wot, when ye do sleep;
We for your sins do both sob and weep,
To pray to God for mercy and for grace,
And thus do we daily with all our whole place.
Wherefore distribute of your temporal wealth,
By which ye may preserve your soul's health.

PARDONER:

What, should ye spend on these flattering liars,
Such as these babbling monks and these friars,
Who do nought daily but babble and lie
And tell ye fables not the worth of a fly;
Such doth this babbling friar here today.
Drive him hence, therefore, in the twenty-devil way!
On us pardoners directly spend your cost,
Because your money never can be lost;
Because there is in our fraternity
For all brothers and sisters who thereof be
Prayers sung reverently, every year,
As he shall know well who cometh there:
At each of the five solemn feasts
A mass and dirge to pray for the good rest
Of the souls of the brothers and sisters all
Of our fraternity in general,
With a hearse there standing well arrayed and dight
And torches and tapers about it burning bright,
And with the bells also solemnly ringing
And priests and clerks devoutly singing.

And furthermore, every night in the year
Twelve poor people are received there
And there have both harbor and food
Which for them is convenient and good.
And furthermore, if there be any other
Who in our fraternity is sister or brother,
Who hereafter happen to fall in decay,
And if ye then chance to come that way
Nigh unto our foresaid place,
Ye shall there tarry for a month's space
And be there kept at the place's cost.
Wherefore now, in the name of the Holy Ghost,
I advise you all, who now here be,
For to be of our fraternity.
Fie on covetise! stick not for a penny
For which ye may have benefits so many.

FRIAR:

I say, wilt thou not yet stint thy clap?
Pull me down the Pardoner with an evil hap!

PARDONER:

Master Friar, I hold it best
To keep your tongue, while ye be in rest.

FRIAR:

I say, one pull the knave off his stool!

PARDONER:

Nay, one pull the friar down like a fool!

FRIAR:

Leave thy railing and babbling of friars,
Or, by Jis, I'sh lug thee by the sweet ears!

PARDONER:

By God, I would thou durst presume it!

FRIAR:

By God, a little thing might make me do it.

PARDONER:

And I curse thy heart, if thou spare—

FRIAR:

> By God, I will not miss thee much, thou slouch;
> And if thou play me such another touch,
> I'sh knock thee on the head, I would thou knew—

PARDONER:

> Marry, that I would see, quoth Blind Hugh.

FRIAR:

> Well, I will begin, and then let me see
> Whether thou darest again interrupt me,
> And what thou would once to it say—

PARDONER:

> Begin and prove whether I will, yea or nay.
>
> > [*The next two speeches are spoken
> > simultaneously.*]

FRIAR:

> And to go forth, where I left right now,
> Our Lord in the Gospel showeth the way how—

PARDONER:

> Because some perhaps will think amiss of me,
> Ye shall now hear the Pope's authority.

FRIAR:

> By Gog's soul, knave, I suffer thee no word—

PARDONER:

> I say, some good body, lend me his sword,
> And I shall teach him, by God's great might,
> How he shall another time learn for to fight!
> I shall make that bald crown of his look red;
> I shall leave him but one ear on his head!

FRIAR:

> But I shall leave thee never an ear, ere I go.

PARDONER:

> Yea, whoreson friar, wilt thou so?
>
> > [*They engage in a fierce fist fight.*]

FRIAR:

> Loose thy hands away from mine ears—

PARDONER:

> Then take thou thy hands away from my hairs!
> Nay, abide, thou whoreson, I am not down yet;
> I trust first to lay thee at my feet.

FRIAR:

> Yea, whoreson, wilt thou scratch and bite?

PARDONER:

> Yea, marry, will I, as long as thou dost smite.
>
> > [*At this point a* PARSON *and a* CONSTABLE,
> > *called* NEIGHBOR PRATT, *enter, in high anger
> > at the use which the preachers are making
> > of the church.*]

PARSON:

> Hold your hands, a vengeance on ye both two,
> That ever ye came hither to make this a-do!
> To pollute my church, a mischief on you light!
> I swear to you, by God's great might,
> Ye shall both repent, every vein of your heart,
> As sore as ye did anything, ere ye depart.

FRIAR:

> Master Parson, I marvel ye will give licence
> To this false knave in this audience,
> To publish his rigmaroles with lies.
> I demanded him, indeed, more than once or twice,
> To hold his peace till that I had done.
> But he would hear no more than the man in the
>   moon.—

PARDONER:

> Why should I suffer thee more than thou me?
> Master Parson gave me licence before thee;
> And I would thou knowest it, I have relics here
> Other manner stuff than thou dost bear.
> I will edify more with the sight of it
> Than will all the prating of holy writ;

Because except that the preacher himself live well,
His preaching will help never a bit,
And I know well that thy living is nought.
Thou art an apostate, if it were well sought.
An homicide thou art, I know well enow,
For myself knew where that thou slew
A wench with thy dagger in a couch;
And yet, as thou say'st in thy sermon, that " no man
    shall touch."

PARSON:

No more of this wrangling in my church!
Curse both your hearts, I'll leave you in the lurch!
Is there any blood shed here between these knaves?
Thanked be God, they had no staves
Nor edged tools, for then all had been wrong.
Well, ye shall sing another song!
Neighbor Pratt, come hither, I you pray—

PRATT:

Why, what is this sharp fray?

PARSON:

I cannot tell you; one knave disdains another;
Wherefore take ye the one, and I shall take the
    other.
We shall dispose of them there as is most con-
    venient,
And such a couple, I think, shall well repent
That ever they met in this church here.
Neighbor, ye be constable; stand ye near,
Take ye that lay knave, and let me alone
With this gentleman; by God and by Saint John,
I shall borrow upon priesthood somewhat;
For I may say to thee, neighbor Pratt,
It is a good deed to punish such and to make
An example to others that they shall not take
Liberties in like fashion as these caitiffs do.

PRATT:

> In good faith, Master Parson, if ye do so,
> Ye do but well to teach them to beware.

PARDONER:

> Master Pratt, I pray ye me to spare;
> For I am sorry for that that is done;
> Wherefore I pray ye forgive me soon,
> For that I have offended within your liberty;
> And by my troth, sir, ye may trust me
> I will never come hither more,
> While I live, and God before!

PRATT:

> Nay, I am once charged with thee,
> Wherefore, by Saint John, thou shalt not escape me
> Till thou hast scoured a pair of stocks.

PARSON:

> Tut, he weeneth all is but mocks!
> Lay hand on him; and come ye on, sir friar,
> Ye shall from me directly have your hire;
> Ye had none such this seven year,
> I swear by God and by our Lady dear.

PARDONER:

> Nay, Master Parson, for God's passion,
> Intreat not me after that fashion;
> For if ye do, it will not be for your honesty.

PARSON:

> Honesty or not, but thou shall see
> What I shall do by and by;
> Make no struggle, come forth soberly;
> For it shall not avail thee, I say.

FRIAR:

> Marry, that shall we try even straightway.
> I defy thee, churl priest, if there be no more than
> thou.

I will not go with thee, I make God a vow.
We shall see first which is the stronger:
God hath sent me bones; I do thee not fear.

PARSON:

Yea, by thy faith, wilt thou be there?
Neighbor Pratt, bring forth that knave,
And thou, sir friar, if thou wilt always rave.

FRIAR:

Nay, churl, I thee defy!
I shall trouble thee first;
Thou shalt go to prison presently;
Let me see, now do thy worst!

> [PRATT *fights fiercely with the* PARDONER *and the* PARSON *with the* FRIAR. *Although the* PARDONER *and the* FRIAR *have hitherto been relatively conciliatory, they get rather the better of the fighting.*]

PARSON:

Help, help, neighbor Pratt, neighbor Pratt,
In the worship of God, help me somewhat!—

PRATT:

Nay, deal as thou canst with that elf,
Because I have enough to do myself.
Alas! for pain I am almost dead;
The red blood so runneth down about my head.
Nay, and thou canst, I pray thee help me.

PARSON:

Nay, by the mass, my friend, it cannot be.
I have more tow on my distaff than I can well spin;
The cursed Friar doth the upper hand win.

FRIAR:

Will ye leave, then, and let us in peace depart?

PARSON *and* PRATT:

Yea, by our Lady, even with all our heart.

FRIAR *and* PARDONER:

Then adieu to the devil, till we come again.

PARSON *and* PRATT:

And a mischief go with you both twain!

> [*The two pair go off with bleeding heads in
> opposite directions as the play ends.*]

SELECTIVE BIBLIOGRAPHY

General Works: E. K. Chambers, *Medieval Stage* (Oxford, 1903). W. Creizenach, *Geschichte des neueren Dramas,* ed. 3, I (Halle, 1920). C. M. Gayley, *Plays of Our Forefathers* (New York, 1909). G. Cohen, *Le Théâtre en France au moyen âge; Le Théâtre religieux* (Paris, 1928); *Le Théâtre profane* (Paris, 1931). A. W. Pollard, *English Miracle Plays, Moralities and Interludes,* ed. 8 (Oxford, 1927). G. Frank, "Introduction to the Study of Mediaeval French Drama," *Essays and Studies in Honor of Carleton Brown* (New York, 1940), pp. 62–78. A. Harbage, *Annals of English Drama, 975–1700* (Philadelphia, 1940). A. Nicoll, *Masks, Mimes, and Miracles* (London, 1931), 135–213.

Collections of Texts: J. Q. Adams, *Chief Pre-Shakespearean Dramas* (Boston, 1924). J. M. Manly, *Specimens of Pre-Shakespearean Drama* (Boston, 1897). K. Young, *Drama of the Medieval Church* (Oxford, 1933). S. B. Hemingway, *English Nativity Plays* (New York, 1909). L. Petit de Julleville, *Répertoire du Théâtre comique en France au moyen âge* (Paris, 1885); *Les Mystères* (Paris, 1880).

Liturgical Drama; Discussion and Texts: K. Young, *Drama of the Medieval Church.* Discussion: P. E. Kretzmann, *Liturgical Element in the Earliest Forms of the Medieval Drama, University of Minnesota Studies in Language and Literature,* No. 4 (1916). A. Jeanroy, *Le Théâtre religieux en France du XIᵉ au XIIIᵉ siècles* (Paris, 1923).

Twelfth Century; Texts: *Hilarii Versus et Ludi,* ed. J. B. Fuller (New York, 1929). *Le Mystère d'Adam,* ed. P. Studer (Manchester, 1918). O. E. Albrecht, *Four Latin Plays of St. Nicholas* (Philadelphia, 1935).

English Miracle Plays: G. R. Coffman, "Miracle Play in England," *Studies in Philology,* XVI (1919), 56–66.

English Mysteries; Discussion: E. L. Swenson, *Inquiry into the Composition and Structure of the Ludus Coventriae, University of Minnesota Studies in Language and Literature,* No. 1 (1914). M. Carey, *Wakefield Group in the Towneley Cycle* (Baltimore, 1930). G. R. Owst, *Literature and Pulpit in Medieval England* (Cambridge, 1933), pp. 471–526. H. A. Watt, "Dramatic Unity of the Secunda Pastorum," *Essays and Studies in Honor of Carleton Brown,* pp. 158–66. M. G. Frampton, "Date of the Flourishing of the Wakefield Master," *PMLA,* L (1935), 631–60. M. H. Marshall, "Dramatic Tradition Established by the Liturgical Plays," *PMLA,* LVI (1941), 962. E. M. Clark, "Liturgical Influences in the Towneley Plays," *Orate Fratres,* XVI (1941), 69. H. W. Wells, "Style in the English Mystery Plays," *JEGP,* XXXVIII (1939), 360.

English Mysteries; Texts: *Chester Plays,* ed. H. Deimling, G. W. Mathews, EETSES (1893, 1916). *Ludus Coventriae,* ed. K. S. Block, EETS (1922). *York Plays,* ed. Lucy T. Smith (Oxford, 1885). *Towneley Plays,* ed. G. England, A. W. Pollard, EETSES (1897).

English Moralities; Discussion: E. N. S. Thompson, *English Moral Plays* (New Haven, 1910). W. R. Mackenzie, *English Moralities from the Point of View of Allegory* (Boston, 1914). W. Farnham, *Medieval Heritage of Elizabethan Tragedy* (1936), pp. 173–212. G. R. Owst, *Literature and Pulpit in Medieval England,* pp. 526–47. W. K. Smart, "The Castle of Perseverance: Place, Date, and a Source," *Manly Anniversary Studies in Language and Literature* (Chicago, 1923), 32–53.

English Moralities; Texts: *Macro Plays,* ed. F. J. Furnivall, A. W. Pollard, EETSES (1904). *Everyman,* ed. K. Goedeke (Hannover, 1865).

Andrieu de la Vigne: E. L. de Kerdaniel, *Un auteur dramatique du quinzième siècle, André de la Vigne* (Paris, 1923).

Secular Drama; Discussion: C. R. Baskervill, "Some Evidence for Early Romantic Plays in England," *MP,* XIV (1916), 229–51. R. S. Loomis, "Chivalric and Dramatic Imitations of

Arthurian Romance." *Mediaeval Studies in Memory of A. Kingsley Porter* (Cambridge, Mass., 1939). G. Frank, "The Beginnings of Comedy in France," *MLR*, XXXI (1936), 377–84. L. Cons, *L'Auteur de la farce de Pathelin, Elliott Monographs* (Princeton, 1926).

Tudor Drama; Discussion: C. F. Tucker Brooke, *Tudor Drama* (Boston, 1911). A. W. Reed, *Early Tudor Drama* (London, 1926). F. S. Boas, *Introduction to Tudor Drama* (Oxford, 1933).

Tudor Drama; Texts: A. Brandl, *Quellen des Weltlichen Dramas in England, Quellen und Forschungen zur Sprach- und Culturgeschichte der Germanischen Völker*, vol. LXXX (Strassburg, 1898).

Henry Medwall; Text: *Fulgens and Lucres*, ed. F. S. Boas, A. W. Reed (Oxford, 1926).

John Heywood; Discussion: R. W. Bolwell, *Life and Works of John Heywood* (New York, 1922). K. Young, "Influence of French Farce upon John Heywood," *MP*, II (1904), 97–124.

John Heywood; Works: R. de la Bère, *John Heywood, Entertainer* (London, 1937). *Dramatic Writings of John Heywood*, ed. J. S. Farmer (London, 1905).

The Medieval Theatre: G. Cohen, *Histoire de la Mise-en-scène dans le Théâtre religieux du moyen âge*, ed. 2 (Paris, 1926). J. C. Stuart, *Stage Decoration in France in the Middle Ages* (New York, 1910). D. Penn, *The Staging of the "Miracles de Nostre Dame par Personnages" of MS. Cangé* (New York, 1933). E. Mâle, *L'art religieux de la fin du moyen âge en France* (Paris, 1908).